Martin Gostelow

Contents

▌*Photo page 1: Emerald Isle*

This Way Ireland

Even if it's your first visit, you will soon feel at home in Ireland. All the better if you have a hint of Irish in your family tree—in which case dozens of genealogical centres are ready to help you trace your ancestry. But wherever you come from, you'll be given a genuine welcome. People talk to each other as a matter of course, in shops, on buses, in the street, and they are remarkably helpful to strangers. Even a simple request for directions can set off a long stream of stories. The Irish are born jokers and gossips, and even if you can't catch all the subtleties, their musical accents will keep you spellbound.

Preserving the Past

The towns and cities are on a human scale, with lively centres and small friendly shops where the staff have the time to attend to you. Places such as Wexford, Galway and Limerick were not bombed in World War II, and whole streets of 18th- and 19th-century buildings survive. Economic expansion brought some ugly redevelopment, especially in Dublin, but now there's a strong movement to preserve the gracious Georgian terraces, often by adapting them as hotels and offices. The villages of the south and west make up an artist's palette of vibrant colours, following a fashion of repainting houses in supposedly traditional shades of lime green, tangerine, custard yellow and blackcurrant. Everywhere, you'll encounter the imprint of history: Neolithic tombs, ruined churches and monasteries, the patterns of abandoned fields, the shells of castles and mansions, and a new interest in interpreting them for today's visitors.

Boom Time

These are great days for the Irish. The country enjoys unprecedented prosperity, with economic growth outpacing its European partners. The boom got under way in earnest in the 1990s. Foreign companies set up factories and businesses, attracted by tax breaks and an educated work force—the school system is recognized as one of Europe's best. The information technology sector has led the way. Many international call centres have moved to Ireland; dial an Internet service provider's helpline or an airline reservation department and you may find yourself talking to someone in Dublin or Waterford.

Even the remote and rugged Aran Isles are experiencing a boom in summer visitors.

The demand for labour became so great that the pattern of emigration was reversed. Instead of leaving in droves, as they have done for almost the whole of the island's history, the Irish have recently been heading home to a land of opportunity.

European Union membership brought benefits too, as Ireland's politicians proved adept at working the system to obtain development grants. You won't travel far without seeing signs announcing some infrastructure project paid for by EU finance. In the remoter parts of the west, where once there was grinding poverty, picturesque but poky cottages have

been replaced by new, often incongruous modern houses, with double-glazing keeping out the draughts. Many of them offer bed and breakfast (B&B) accommodation—in parts of the west of Ireland there's hardly a house that doesn't display its Tourist Board-approved shamrock sign outside. As a result, you'll have no problem finding somewhere to stay, in contrast with Dublin where demand for hotel rooms can often outstrip the supply.

Coast and Countryside

This being an island, water is a recurring theme. You are never more than 112 km (70 miles) from the sea, and usually within sight of one of its 800 lakes and rivers. To simplify the geography, Ireland is like a shallow saucer, the rim representing the mountains. The coastline is heavily indented, rising from glorious sweeps of sand to dramatic headlands. In the centre, the Midlands is an area of pastures, lakes and lazy rivers and includes the Great Bog, with its own strange appeal.

City Lights

Big families are still the norm in rural areas, but opportunities are limited so the young flock to the cities. On a Saturday night it can seem as if they are all out at the same time, crowding the streets or packing into the pubs, bars or clubs. There is such a bewildering number of places to drink in every town that it's hard to understand how they can all make a living. The pub is unquestionably the focus of Ireland's social life, serving as a debating society, dating agency, dealing room, dance hall and general home-from-home. If the atmosphere or style of music in one doesn't suit you, just move on until you find somewhere more to your taste. It's easy to meet the locals, but be warned, what starts out as a quiet evening can turn into a contest to see who can tell the tallest tale. Drinks flow ever more freely as complete strangers become your greatest friends and the humour grows ever broader. It's all part of the famous "crack" (or *craic*), a term that has no translation—and doesn't need one, once you've experienced it.

FACTS AND FIGURES

Lying between Great Britain and the Atlantic Ocean, Ireland is roughly 480 km (300 miles) long from north to south and up to 275 km (171 miles) from east to west, not counting the many small offshore islands scattered round the coast. Since 1922, it has been divided into the 26 counties of the Republic of Ireland (Eire) and the 6 counties of Northern Ireland, part of the United Kingdom.

Republic of Ireland
Area: 70,000 sq km
(27,000 sq miles)
Population: 3.7 million
Dublin: 480,000
(metropolitan area: 1.1 million)
Cork: 130,000

Northern Ireland
Area: 14,000 sq km
(5,400 sq miles)
Population: 1.6 million
Belfast: 300,000
(metropolitan area: 500,000)
Londonderry (Derry): 65,000

Prehistory

The first humans arrived in Ireland about 9,000 years ago, probably to hunt in the forests that covered most of it after the end of the last Ice Age. They must have come by boat, because the land bridge from Britain had been broken by then. (This is why there are no snakes or moles; they didn't make it before the sea severed the link.)

Pollen analysis and other archaeological evidence show that by 4000 BC, people had started to clear the forests, plant crops and raise domesticated animals. Soon after that, they began to build stone tombs, which became more and more elaborate. From a few boulders covered with earth, they developed into portal tombs (or dolmens) with three large stones supporting a capstone weighing up to 100 tonnes, and reached a peak around 3000 BC with massive passage tombs such as Newgrange. In these, a narrow tunnel leads to a tall, roofed chamber, and the whole structure is covered with earth or stones to form a huge mound.

A weather-carved face in Yeats's land of "terrible beauty".

Bronze and copper tools appeared before 2000 BC, and the gorgeous gold collars and bracelets to be seen in the National Museum in Dublin were made in the later Bronze Age, from 1200–700 BC. And wherever you go in Ireland, you'll come across stone circles and tall monoliths from the same era.

Who were the Celts?

That's a question to start an argument among the experts. It used to be thought that the Iron Age came to Ireland with the Celts, a people who spread from central to western Europe in the 5th century BC. Now, the more popular theory holds that the techniques of iron smelting and working were adopted by the existing population; the culture known as Celtic was imported but there was no great wave of immigration. Whatever the truth, it's clear that powerful kingdoms grew up in several parts of Ireland, probably enlarging their territory with iron weapons and building stone forts for defence. By 100 BC, ceremonial sites such as the Hill of Tara and Navan Fort were the scenes of important rituals, described in sagas preserved by storytellers until the dawn of written history. 7

The Romans conquered most of Britain in the 1st century AD and held it for 350 years, but they never tried to occupy Ireland. Instead, they engaged in trade; many Roman coins and artefacts have been found in southeast Ireland, as well as the foundations of a trading post near Howth, north of Dublin.

Christian Conversion

One of Ireland's exports had been slaves, but when Rome's power waned, the traffic switched direction—Irish raiders seized captives in Britain. Among them was the future St Patrick, who spent seven years in Ulster as a cowherd, but then escaped and went to Gaul (France). He was ordained as a priest, and returned to Ireland in about the year 432 on a mission to convert its people to Christianity. From his base in Armagh (still Ireland's ecclesiastical capital), he and his followers were remarkably successful. In contrast to the rest of northern Europe, there were no bloodbaths and no martyrs, perhaps owing to St Patrick's shrewdness in gaining the support of local kings and chiefs. Once they were converted, their people followed.

Strong monastic orders grew up in the 6th and 7th centuries, and soon shook off any influence from Britain or Gaul, which had fallen under the rule of pagan barbarians. Ireland began to send out its own missionaries, Colmcille (St Columba) founding a monastery on Iona, an island off northwest Scotland, which led to the conversion of Scotland and northern England.

The monasteries became rich, and it may have been news of easy pickings that tempted Scandinavian Vikings to plunder the coasts of northern Europe. Their first attack on Ireland took place in 795, when several island sites were sacked. In the ensuing years the raiding fleets grew bigger and nowhere was safe. In 840, instead of heading home at the end of summer, a large group of Vikings from Norway spent the winter near Lough Neagh in Ulster. In the years that followed they built settlements where Dublin, Wexford, Waterford, Cork and Limerick now stand, all with good sheltered harbours. The Irish resisted; the invaders were thrown out of Dublin for a few years and eventually defeated in 1014 by an Irish army under High King Brian Boru, although he was killed at the moment of victory.

Norman Invasions

In the 12th century, the land-hungry Normans who had seized England and Wales started to look across the Irish Sea. The only Englishman ever to be pope, Adrian IV, was persuaded to name Henry II of England as "Lord of Ireland", but he was too busy in France to make the title a reality. Then came an internal dispute between two Irish kings, which was to change the course of history. Diarmaid (Dermot) MacMurrough King of Leinster had abducted the wife of a supporter of the High King, and had been forced to flee from Ireland. He went to the Norman Earl of Pembroke, known as "Strongbow", offering him his daughter in marriage and to make him his heir, in exchange for help in regaining his kingdom.

In 1170, Strongbow landed near Waterford and quickly captured the town. The promised wedding took place and the invasion force moved on to seize Dublin. When Diarmaid conveniently died in 1171, Strongbow inherited the crown of Leinster. Now King Henry decided to take charge. He crossed to Ireland and made grants of land to his supporters, leaving the actual conquest of it to them. Some Irish lords were left in possession of their lands in exchange for declaring their allegiance. For himself, Henry kept Dublin and its fertile hinterland, an area which became known as the "Pale", where English rule was most secure.

Now the Norman lords applied the methods which had been so successful in England. They built castles and granted parcels of land to their followers in exchange for support; their heavily armed soldiers enforced the dispossession of the existing owners, and the peasants had no choice but to work for the new masters. Later, immigrants were brought from England in the first of many "plantation" schemes; new fortified towns were built and the Church came under the control of Anglo-Norman bishops and abbots. Even so, the conquest of Ireland was far from complete. The far west was never pacified, and the invaders even suffered some heavy defeats at the hands of Irish Gaelic forces.

After the Black Death killed a third of the population in the mid-14th century, manpower was so short that the Anglo-Norman lords recruited Irish soldiers and formed alliances with Irish chieftains, frequently cemented by intermarriage. By the 15th century, most of Ireland beyond the Pale was ruled by powerful Anglo-Irish magnates who paid little heed to Dublin, and still less to their nominal sovereign in London.

Wars of Religion

Following the Reformation in England, Henry VIII took the title of King of Ireland and began closing monasteries and confis- 9 cating Church property, just as he had done in England. But in devoutly Catholic Ireland there was fierce resentment and a succession of failed uprisings, culminating in 1607 with the "Flight of the Earls" (of Tyrconnell and Tyrone) and their supporters to exile in mainland Europe after the defeat of a rebellion in Ulster. Their land was confiscated and given to settlers from Scotland and England, resulting in the Protestant majority in Northern Ireland that persists to this day.

Civil war in England between the king's supporters and those of Parliament triggered yet another rising in Ireland as the dispossessed tried to regain their lands. Many Anglo-Irish and Irish lords joined the Royalist cause and held out against the Parliamentary forces until Oliver Cromwell, after the execution of Charles I, crossed over to Ireland in 1649, determined to crush all resistance. Drogheda and Wexford were besieged and stormed, many of the defenders were killed and the survivors sentenced to virtual slavery in Caribbean sugar plantations.

Landowners who had opposed Parliament had their property seized and given to Cromwell's soldiers and financiers.

Restoration

The death of Cromwell was followed in 1660 by the Restoration of the monarchy under Charles II. The Catholic James II succeeded his brother, but he was soon deposed in the Revolution of 1688 and replaced by his son-in-law, the Protestant William of Orange. James sought the support of Louis XIV of France and was given some troops and money. Landing at Kinsale in 1689, he was welcomed as the rightful king and soon set up his court in Dublin. Only the Protestants in the North opposed his forces; Derry withstood a siege of 105 days until it was relieved by sea. The event is celebrated by the Protestant community still today. William assembled an army and, determined to retake the whole of Ireland, landed near Belfast in June 1690. Marching south, he routed

James's smaller Irish and French army on 12 July in the Battle of the Boyne, although the war dragged on in the west for another year. A new Protestant Parliament was set up in Dublin; Catholics were denied the vote and forbidden to buy land or enter the professions. Only members of the Protestant Episcopalian Church of Ireland—around one-tenth of the population—had full political rights. In the rural areas there was dire poverty and many people emigrated to the American colonies, not only from the Catholic south and west but the predominantly Presbyterian north.

The Struggle for Independence

The American War of Independence turned Irish minds to thoughts of freedom, and the French Revolution was a further impetus. Protestants resented the restrictions that London had imposed on Irish trade and negotiated better terms, and Catholics were given the vote in an effort to buy their loyalty. In 1791, the Society of United Irishmen was formed by Presbyterian and Catholic intellectuals led by Theobald Wolfe Tone, to call for a fairer system of electing the Irish Parliament, but when war with France broke out in 1794, the Society was banned. Wolfe Tone sought French help, but two attempts at invasion failed, he was captured and condemned to death.

The British government's reaction to Irish discontent was to push through the Act of Union in 1800, forming the United Kingdom of Great Britain and Ireland. The Irish parliament was abolished and Dublin became a political backwater. A young lawyer, Daniel O'Connell, was elected to the House of Commons in London, but as a Catholic, he could not take his seat. The outcry was so great that the law was modified, and he entered Parliament in 1829. He began a long campaign for the repeal of the Act of Union, but did not live to see its eventual success.

In September 1845 blight struck the potato, the staple food of the Irish peasantry, on farms in the southeast. Over the next few years, the potato crop failed successively nationwide, resulting in widespread famine. One million people died of starvation and disease; another million fled the country aboard the infamous "coffin ships", beginning a steady flow of emigrants that was not stanched till over a century later.

The British government's inadequate and ineffective measures to relieve the famine intensified resentment among the Irish people and increased their determination to break away 11 from British dominion. By 1874, most of the Irish seats in Parliament were won by supporters of Home Rule, but the party suffered a setback when its leader, Charles Stewart Parnell, was disgraced in a divorce case. Despite the support of Gladstone, the British prime minister, bills to introduce Home Rule were defeated. Nationalist feeling in Ireland led to the formation of new political organizations such as *Sinn Féin*, ("Ourselves") and the Irish Republican Brotherhood (IRB). In 1912, the Home Rule Bill was finally passed, but the Unionists who were in the majority in Ulster campaigned against it and 100,000 Ulster Volunteers declared themselves ready to resist its imposition. In Dublin, an Irish Volunteer force was formed and an arms race between the two militias began.

In September 1914, the Home Rule Bill became law, but with the outbreak of the World War I, it was suspended until hostilities should cease. The IRB and the armed groups began to plan an uprising. On 24 April 1916, Easter Monday, their leaders declared an Irish republic and several public buildings in Dublin were seized. But the insurgents were too few, and after a week of street fighting, the survivors surrendered. Fifteen of their leaders were convicted of treason and shot, an act of repression which only increased nationalist support. In the 1918 general election, Sinn Féin won most of the Irish seats, except in the north. But they refused to sit in the London parliament and met in Dublin instead, as the *Dáil Éireann*, or Irish Assembly. Fighting broke out between their armed supporters, the Irish Republican Army (IRA), and British forces, including the militia called the Black and Tans after the colour of their uniforms.

Partition

After two years of raids, murders and reprisals, Britain wearied of the bloodshed; a treaty was signed in 1921 creating an Irish Free State as part of the British Commonwealth. Six of the nine counties of Ulster in which there was a Unionist majority remained in the United Kingdom. The treaty bitterly divided the nationalists. Some saw it as the best deal available and supported the new government headed by Michael Collins; to others, led by Eamon de Valera, it was a betrayal. A vicious civil war broke out in which Collins was assassinated. The government reacted by executing those who carried arms against it and by 1923 an uneasy peace was established.

At first, de Valera's *Fianna Fáil* party boycotted the new Irish

Parliament, the Dáil, but later entered it and in 1932 won enough seats to form the government. In 1937, the Irish Free State was renamed *Éire* and became effectively a republic. It stayed out of World War II, while Northern Ireland was fully involved—German aircraft repeatedly bombed Belfast with its shipyards and aircraft factories.

The 1960s brought industrial expansion in the Republic, a process given a boost when it joined the European Economic Community (now the European Union) in 1973, at the same time as the UK. A more outward-looking Ireland became a regular contributor to peace-keeping forces in the world's trouble spots. In 1979, the historic step was taken to break the link with the pound sterling, creating the Irish pound or *punt*.

The Northern Question

Meanwhile, trouble had been brewing in Northern Ireland. The minority Catholics had long complained about discrimination over jobs, housing and political rights. In 1968, resentment boiled over in a series of marches and demonstrations. Nationalists and Unionists clashed in the streets and British troops were sent to separate them. In 1971, the Provisional IRA began a campaign of bombing and shooting, initially aimed at the security forces but later spreading to civilian targets, with the intention of wearing down British resolve and sickening the public of bloodshed. But Britain would not abandon its commitment to keep Northern Ireland in the UK as long as a majority in the province wished it. By the 1990s there was stalemate—a low level of violence and no apparent hope of a solution. Recognizing that a new approach was needed, the British and Irish governments held talks, at first in secret and then openly, with the political wings of the illegal armed groups (or "paramilitaries"), including the IRA. Those groups declared a ceasefire, temporary at first but later proclaimed permanent.

Tortuous negotiations between the political parties in Northern Ireland led to the 1999 Good Friday Agreement for the setting up of a power-sharing system of self-government. Republicans saw this as a step towards a united Ireland, but Unionists had no intention of acceding to such an outcome. A major bone of contention was the refusal of the paramilitaries to give up their weapons, leaving an uneasy armed truce. A solution still looks a long way off, but the hope must be that people of all persuasions, having enjoyed a few years of peace, won't give it up lightly.   13

On the Scene

Despite the attractions of the cities, you'll probably be as keen as most travellers to get out and enjoy the magnificent coastal and mountain scenery. Our sightseeing section begins with Dublin and moves clockwise round the island, finishing with Northern Ireland. Few visitors can take the time to do all that; distances may look short on the map, but you are always likely to be diverted and delayed by some delightful surprises. Don't restrict yourself to main highways; much of the charm is hidden away down the back roads.

DUBLIN

City Centre, Early Dublin, North of the Liffey, Glasnevin, Southern Suburbs

Ireland's capital is one of Europe's success stories, and proud of it. Ambitious schemes have transformed run-down areas, and gracious 18th-century buildings, long neglected, have been turned to imaginative new uses. From financial services to tourism to rock music, business is booming. A notably young and cosmopolitan crowd gathers in the cafés and pubs to drink and gossip, for this is still at heart a big, friendly village. One-way systems, pedestrian streets and parking restrictions mean that it's best seen on foot. If you have a car, find a safe place to park, and leave it.

City Centre

The city's most famous thoroughfare, O'Connell Street, crosses the River Liffey by way of O'Connell Bridge. A massive monument to "The Liberator", Daniel O'Connell (1775–1847) stands just to the north of it. The wide street was laid out in the 18th century, like a long version of a Georgian square. On the west side, the General Post Office, or GPO, was seized by the insurgents at the start of the Easter Ris-

Ha'penny Bridge was built in 1816 and named for the toll charged to cross over the Liffey.

ing of 1916. A week later, with the building in flames after shelling, they were forced to surrender. The statues lining the central reservation include Father Mathew, founder of the temperance movement and, at the north end, Charles Stewart Parnell (1846–91), leader of the Home Rule campaign. Reclining in a fountain, the plump figure of Anna Livia Plurabelle, James Joyce's spirit of the Liffey, is mocked by Dubliners as "The Floozy in the Jacuzzi".

The Abbey Theatre on Abbey Street stages plays by Irish writers, both classics and new. East of O'Connell Bridge a green copper dome tops the elegant 1770s Custom House, by James Gandon, architect of some of Dublin's finest buildings. It was set ablaze in the 1921 fighting, when the original interior was destroyed. Now restored, it houses an exhibition on Gandon's life and work. From the Custom House to the docks, the north bank of the Liffey was transformed in the 1990s from derelict wasteland into Dublin's burgeoning financial district.

South of O'Connell Bridge is the curved and colonnaded wall of the 18th-century Bank of Ireland, home of the Irish Parliament until it was abolished by the 1800 Act of Union. The old Commons Chamber has long been split into offices, but it is still possible to see the former House of Lords.

Trinity College

Across College Green from the Bank of Ireland is the impressive gateway of Trinity College, the University of Dublin, founded in 1592 on the orders of Queen Elizabeth I. Until 1873 only Protestants were admitted, and even when the law was changed, the Roman Catholic hierarchy would not allow Catholics to attend, a restriction that was only relaxed in the 1950s.

Over the centuries the college expanded into a complex of fine buildings set around quadrangles, green lawns and playing fields, an extraordinary island amid the city streets. The area teems with students, but it's usually open to the public too. The main gate is

1

THE MOST PRECIOUS MANUSCRIPT The **Book of Kells**, kept in Trinity College Library, Dublin, is a magnificently illuminated edition of the Gospels in Latin, written and embellished by monks in the 9th century.

flanked by statues of the political thinker Edmund Burke and the playwright Oliver Goldsmith. Other Trinity College alumni include Jonathan Swift, Oscar Wilde and Samuel Beckett.

Student guides conduct tours, or you can make your own way through Parliament (or Front) Square and Library Square to College Park. The magnificent Old Library, built between 1712 and 1732, originally consisted of the open Colonnades at ground level and the Long Room upstairs which was the actual library. Then, in 1801, it was granted the right, along with the British Library and the Bodleian, Oxford, to a free copy of any book published in Britain or Ireland. Ever since, the demand for shelf space has grown inexorably. First the Long Room was given its barrel-vaulted roof and upper gallery bookcases: it houses 200,000 of the oldest books. Then the Colonnades were walled in to make more space, and now the Library has many buildings on other sites.

The Colonnades have been turned into a shop and exhibition area, and here in subdued light is displayed the early 9th-century *Book of Kells*. This pinnacle of Irish art is a Latin manuscript of the four Gospels, embellished with complex designs. Its name comes from the vanished monastery of Kells in County Meath, but it may have been written on Iona off the west coast of Scotland, founded by the Irish missionary St Columba. In the same room, the *Book of Durrow* may date from the mid-7th century.

Grafton Street

Emerging at Trinity's main gate and turning left into Grafton Street, look among the pedestrians for the bronze statue of the city's mascot, Molly Malone, with generous cleavage and a barrow laden with shellfish.

In Dublin's fair city
Where the girls are so pretty
I first set my eyes on sweet
  Molly Malone.
She wheeled her wheelbarrow
Through streets broad
  and narrow
Crying "cockles and mussels
Alive, alive, O!"

This is Dublin's prime shopping area. South of the Nassau Street crossing, it's closed to traffic, and entertainers from classical musicians to rock groups compete to catch your ear.

St Stephen's Green

Grafton Street leads to St Stephen's Green, a huge square and park filled by lawns, flowerbeds and a lake. The many statues include Sir Arthur Guinness, who gave the park to the people of Dublin, W. B. Yeats by Henry Moore, and a strange effigy of

17

James Joyce with his legs twisted into a coil and the tribute "He dismantled the English language and put it together again so that it became music." At the northeast corner, a tall bronze figure of Wolfe Tone stands opposite the historic Shelbourne Hotel.

Some of the fine houses that lined the squares and streets of Georgian Dublin have been lost, although many still survive—if only as offices. To see what a gracious interior could have been like, visit Newman House at Nos. 85 and 86 St Stephen's Green. A block east, Fitzwilliam Square (1825) has some of the best-kept houses, many of them doctors' consulting rooms.

Merrion Square

For a century and a half this was the best address in Dublin. Daniel O'Connell once lived at No. 58, W. B. Yeats at No. 82, the Wilde family at No. 1. Every weekend a big open-air art show and sale is held in the square. Between Merrion Square and Kildare Street, a single city block is full of riches: the National Gallery, National Museum, National Library and Natural History Museum, not to mention Leinster House, the home of the Irish Parliament.

Dublin's doors reflect an era of gracious living.

National Gallery of Ireland

On the west side of Merrion Square, a statue of George Bernard Shaw marks the entrance to the National Gallery (he left it one-third of his estate). It is hard to pick highlights, but the great names include Fra Angelico, Rubens and Rembrandt (*Rest on the Flight into Egypt*) among many Dutch masters, and a strong Spanish School, including Velázquez and Goya (the sensuous *El Sueño*, The Dream). Reynolds and Gainsborough lead the English portraitists, but this being Ireland's show, look for William Leech *(The Goose Girl)* and William Orpen's extraordinary *The Holy Well* (1916). John Butler Yeats, father of W. B. Yeats, Lily Yeats and Jack B. Yeats, painted portraits of his children, which hang near a large collection of Jack B. Yeats's own work, from the exciting *Liffey Swim* to his mystic late pictures.

National Museum of Ireland

The star attractions are the breathtaking gold ornaments from the Bronze Age and Iron Age, found in hoards, peat bogs or during 19th-century excavations for railways. Look out for the torcs from 1000 BC, twisted from ribbons of gold, huge gold belts and the 8th-century BC Gleninsheen gold collar and armlets. From the Iron Age, see the delicate little gold boat with 16 tiny oars, from around the 1st century AD.

The 8th-century Ardagh Chalice of beaten silver decorated with gold filigree was found under a stone in 1868 by a boy pulling up potatoes, and the Tara Brooch was picked up on a beach. Made of silver with gold filigree and amber, it also dates from the 8th century.

"BLOOMSDAY"

Even in Dublin, few people have read James Joyce's *Ulysses*, but plenty have heard of it. Each year on June 16, the date in 1904 when the events of the novel take place, there are dramatizations and readings, rarely omitting Molly Bloom's erotic daydream ("and yes I said yes I will Yes"). Parties follow the footsteps of the protagonist Leopold Bloom from Prospect Cemetery to the banks of the Liffey. They head for Grafton Street, locate Davy Byrne's restaurant and continue to the National Library, where Bloom sees his wife's lover, Blazes Boylan. There's no need to wait for June 16; maps of the circuit are sold in bookshops, and plaques in the pavement mark strategic points along the way.

19

The bronze Shrine of St Patrick's Bell (12th century) is decorated with gold and silver-gilt in the Norse style which influenced Irish work. The 5th-century iron and bronze bell, which the shrine was made to house, survives, too.

Less eye-catching but still fascinating are the flint, bone, stone and bronze tools, weapons and ornaments from the time of the earliest known human settlement in Ireland, around 7000 BC, right up to the modern era. The upstairs galleries display Irish silver, textiles, glass, and musical instruments.

National Library

Backing onto the National Gallery is the National Library in Kildare Street. Every famous Irish writer seems to have worked under the dome of the first-floor Reading Room since it was opened in 1890.

Early Dublin

The Vikings probably settled on the bank of the Liffey where Wood Quay is now; the Viking Adventure exhibition gives an idea of what life might have been like. This area remained the city's focus until the early 18th century, but then the whole district was neglected when the Georgian streets and squares to the east became the fashionable areas to live.

Dublin Castle

The 12th-century Norman castle was replaced by a new one in the 14th century as the threat of rebellion never went away. Early attempts to dislodge the Normans were echoed in the 1916 Rising when a unit of the Irish Citizen Army attacked the castle but failed to break in. Less than six years later, the last viceroy handed the keys to Michael Collins, head of government of the new Irish Free State.

The complex of buildings you see today is largely an 18th-century reconstruction, with recent additions made for meetings of European Union ministers. Visitors can stroll in the Castle Yards, but to see the State Apartments, check in at the tour entrance in the Upper Yard. Usually on show are St Patrick's Hall, where the Knights of the Order of St Patrick used to be invested, the Wedgwood Room, the Picture Gallery with portraits of British viceroys, and the gilded Throne Room where they sat on ceremonial occasions. The Gothic revival Chapel Royal is decorated outside with 100 stone heads of characters from Irish history, including St Kevin and Jonathan Swift.

Christ Church Cathedral

By a quirk of history, the older churches in the Republic belong to the minority Protestant Church of Ireland, including Dublin's two great medieval cathedrals.

Christ Church Cathedral was started by the Vikings, but in 1173, soon after the Norman conquest, a new church was begun on the site, by order of Strongbow and Archbishop (later Saint) Laurence O'Toole. Most of the present building dates from the 12th and 13th centuries, but its appearance today owes a lot to renovations in the 1870s.

Near the entrance is a tomb still called Strongbow's, though the effigy of a knight dates from the 14th century, much later than his time. Down in the crypt, rough stone pillars and Norman arches support the massive structure.

St Patrick's Cathedral

A short walk south from Christ Church, St Patrick's was consecrated in 1192. The reason a second cathedral was begun soon after the first lies in the rivalry between Ireland's monasteries and the separate hierarchy of bishops. In the southwest corner, the enormous Boyle Monument was erected by Richard Boyle, Earl of Cork, in 1633. Painted figures represent the earl and his second wife, with eleven of their children.

At the west end of the nave is the chapterhouse door with a roughly sawn hole like a letter-

CLOSE RELATIONS

Swift seems to have first met his "Stella" in England when she was 8 and he was 22. He paid for her education and later asked her to come over to Ireland. Their relationship inspired endless gossip. Some said they had secretly married, but they did not live together and there is no evidence to support the story. In 1728 Stella died, and Swift sat night after night in the cold cathedral, apparently composing letters to her.

box. The story goes that the Earl of Kildare cut it in 1492, and reached through to grasp the hand of the Earl of Ormonde, who had taken refuge there after they had a violent argument. In so "chancing his arm" he gave a phrase to the language.

Jonathan Swift, satirist and author of *Gulliver's Travels,* was dean of St Patrick's from 1713 until his death in 1745. His bust is in the nave to the right of the entrance, and his grave and that of his beloved "Stella" (Esther Johnson) lie side by side near the wall. Swift's pulpit, table and chair stand in the north transept.

In Swift's time, parts of the cathedral were in ruins, and had been since Cromwell's troopers 21 had stabled their horses here. Only massive restoration in the 19th century saved St Patrick's: the chief benefactors, members of the Guinness family, are commemorated in statues and in the north transept window.

Marsh's Library

Behind St Patrick's, this was Ireland's first public library (1701) and it still functions as one. The original oak bookcases with their carved and lettered gables have been beautifully restored, along with the cages where readers were locked in to ensure they didn't steal the precious volumes.

St Audoen's Church

Across the street to the west of Christ Church, this Norman church houses an exhibition on Celtic Ireland. In an adjoining alley, the restored St Audoen's Arch is the only gateway to survive from the 13th-century city wall. The narrow streets west of here used to be one of Dublin's more squalid slums, The Liberties. Now cleaned up, its streets are lined with antique and junk shops, bargain outlets and street traders' carts.

Temple Bar

One small street has given its name to Dublin's equivalent of the Left Bank in Paris, though here it's the right bank. From Christ Church Cathedral at one end to the Bank of Ireland at the other, Temple Bar has a host of wine bars, pubs and restaurants, as well as music, film, art and book centres, and free events in the evenings. Many streets have been designated pedestrian only.

Guinness Brewery

West of the centre and south of the River Liffey, the brewery is one of Europe's biggest. More than half the beer drunk in Ireland is produced here, most famously the dark stout which Arthur Guinness began brewing in 1759. A World of Guinness exhibition centre is housed in the old hop store. You're invited to sample a glass in the Old Dublin Bar.

Until the 1960s, both the Grand Canal, which widens into a harbour south of the brewery, and the River Liffey were used to bring in barley and hops. Some of the product went out by the same route, a nice gentle way for it to travel which gave rise to a theory that "Canal" Guinness was the best of the lot. (To learn about canal trips, go to the Waterways Visitor Centre at Grand Canal basin, east of Trinity College.)

Royal Hospital

South of the Liffey, next to Heuston railway station, the Royal Hospital was built in 1684 as a home for retired soldiers. Ar-

Professors in full academic regalia beneath the portals of Trinity College.

ranged around a spacious arcaded courtyard, it is the finest 17th-century building in Ireland. Since 1991 it has been the home of the Irish Museum of Modern Art and its often controversial shows.

Kilmainham Jail

Nearby, on South Circular Road stands the grim, grey jail where many Irish patriots were incarcerated. The guides can tell you where most of the famous prisoners were held, particularly the leaders of the 1916 Easter Rising before they were taken out to one of the yards to be shot. A plaque on the wall bears their names and the dates of their deaths.

North of the Liffey

At the top of O'Connell Street, Parnell Square encloses a complex of buildings including the former Assembly Rooms, a fashionable social venue in the 18th century. Part is now a cinema, and an extension houses the Gate Theatre. In the northwest corner, a Garden of Remembrance honours all those who died fighting for Ireland's freedom.

Dublin Writers' Museum

On Parnell Square North, with the Irish Writers' Centre next door, the museum pays tribute to the Irish-born giants of literature. The first display room deals with 23 the earlier figures: Swift, Goldsmith and Sheridan, Maria Edgeworth, Wilde and Shaw. The second room spans the period from the 1890s onwards: J.M. Synge, Yeats and his circle, Joyce, O'Casey and Beckett and many others, through photographs, letters and memorabilia.

Hugh Lane Municipal Gallery of Modern Art

In the 1762 Charlemont House, the gallery houses pictures left to Dublin by Sir Hugh Lane, an art lover who was drowned in 1915 when the *Lusitania* was sunk by a German submarine. And what pictures! Monet's *Vétheuil in Sunshine and Snow*, the luminous *Jour d'Eté* by Berthe Morisot and *Eva Gonzales* by Manet. Watts and Burne-Jones represent the Pre-Raphaelites, and there are vivid Irish scenes by Lavery, Leech and Orpen.

King's Inns

West of Parnell Square, the classical King's Inns were designed by James Gandon but not finished until 1816, after his death. Home of the Irish legal profession, the name comes from the original 16th-century inns where the lawyers actually lived.

Smithfield

The Smithfield district used to be synonymous with produce markets and distilleries, but redevelopment has changed all that. The scent of malted barley has long since faded away, as production was moved to Midleton, Co. Cork. The story is told in the Old Jameson Distillery, with relics, a film and maybe a little drop to taste.

Gandon's Four Courts building of 1802 took its name from the courts of law it was built to house. There's a fine view of the city from the upper gallery of the rotunda.

Facing the river to the west, the majestic Collins Barracks date from 1704. After long neglect, they have been restored and now serve as an annex of the National Museum.

Phoenix Park

The biggest walled city park in Europe could easily hold the entire population of Dublin without overcrowding (and practically did, when Pope John Paul II celebrated mass). Near the southeastern gate, a colossal obelisk, over 60 m (200 ft) high, commemorates Wellington's victories in India and the Napoleonic Wars. Although born in Dublin, the Iron Duke ungraciously discounted his Irish origins, remarking that a man may be born in a stable, but that doesn't make him a horse!

On the northern edge of the park, the official residence of the

President of Ireland is the same Georgian house where British viceroys once held court, within earshot of the calls of the animals in Dublin Zoo.

Glasnevin

About 3 km (2 miles) north at Glasnevin, Dublin's Botanic Gardens and the vast Prospect Cemetery almost adjoin, but their entrances are quite far apart.

National Botanic Gardens

The gardens were established at the end of the 18th century when expeditions brought back seeds and specimens from every part of the globe. The cast-iron glasshouses date from the 1840s. Separate sections of the gardens feature herbs, roses, cacti and bonsai.

Prospect Cemetery

Also known as Glasnevin, the cemetery is the burial place of many of Ireland's heroes. Near the main gates, Daniel O'Connell lies in a crypt under the round tower; Parnell's prominent grave is not far away. The remains of Sir Roger Casement (1864–1916) were brought from London and reburied opposite the gate in 1965. To the right of the entrance, in the nationalists' plot, are the graves of Eamon de Valera, Constance (Gore-Booth) Markievicz (1868–1927) and others who fought for Irish freedom.

Southern Suburbs

Southeast from St Stephen's Green, Leeson Street's discos and clubs are where night owls go when everywhere else has closed. Across the Grand Canal, Ballsbridge is a district of leafy streets and elegant houses. It became the fashionable area to live in late Victorian times, and most foreign embassies are located here. The Royal Dublin Society (RDS) has its extensive grounds right in the middle, the venue of concerts, exhibitions and the famous Dublin Horse Show.

Chester Beatty Library and Gallery of Oriental Art

Filling a mansion at 20, Shrewsbury Road, it largely comprises the collection gathered by Sir Alfred Chester Beatty, a Canadian mining magnate who came to live in Dublin in the 1950s. He died in 1968 and left his treasures to Ireland: Babylonian clay tablets from 2500 BC, biblical texts, early printed books, Chinese seals and Mughal miniatures.

Dun Laoghaire

"Dunleary", as it is pronounced, became a suburb of Dublin when the railway arrived, but it retains a distinct character as a fishing port, ferry terminal and yachting centre. The Maritime Museum in the Mariners' Church has some interesting relics and ship models.

EXCURSIONS FROM DUBLIN

Howth, Malahide, Drogheda, Boyne Valley, Kells, Trim, Castletown House, Kildare, Punchestown, Russborough House, Sandycove, Powerscourt

The DART suburban railway, coach or car will quickly whisk you away from the hustle of the city centre to the tranquil surroundings of a stately home set in beautiful gardens, to some of Ireland's most ancient and historic sites or to picturesque seaside villages and towns.

Howth

The Howth peninsula stands like a sentinel on the north side of Dublin Bay; take a walk to the top for a fine view. The town's restaurants and hotels make it a favourite weekend spot for Dubliners, and the harbour is a haven for pleasure craft. On a calm day, excursion boats take trips to Ireland's Eye, a rocky island which was an early monastic settlement. Now uninhabited, Ireland's Eye is a bird sanctuary, but visitors can stroll and picnic.

Largely Georgian, Howth Castle is still lived in by descendants of the Norman lord who took the peninsula in battle from its Norse and Irish defenders. The Transport Museum Society of Ireland uses some of the outbuildings to keep its collection, from trams, fire engines and armoured cars to humble horse-drawn bread vans.

Malahide

When Henry II visited Ireland in 1171, he gave land to Richard Talbot, who put up a defensive tower which has been augmented over the centuries to create the present Malahide Castle. Its wooded grounds and vast lawns are popular with Dublin families, who come for a stroll or to fly kites. Tours start in the original tower, in a 16th-century panelled room and move on to much loftier rooms added in the 18th century. Many pictures are on loan from the National Portrait Collection, among them a Van Dyck of the children of Charles I, and others by Rubens, Kneller and Lely. The medieval Great Hall, complete with minstrels' gallery, is a rare survival in an Irish house. Upstairs is the children's room, with dolls, an ancient tricycle and lace robes; another bedroom has the actor David Garrick's bed.

The Fry Model Railway, in an outbuilding, is one of the biggest and best set-ups you'll ever see, with model trains from Irish railway history, Dublin trams and barges loading barrels of Guinness on the Liffey as they did until 1960.

Drogheda

A Viking settlement at the first crossing point of the River Boyne, Drogheda was later fortified by the Anglo-Normans. Oliver Cromwell and his army besieged the town in 1649. When the walls were at last breached, 2,000 people (by Cromwell's own admission) were massacred. The principal relic of the defences is the twin-tower St Lawrence's Gate, a 13th-century barbican which stood in front of the wall.

In the Gothic revival Catholic St Peter's Church on West Street, the embalmed head of St Oliver Plunkett is displayed in a glass case. He was an Archbishop of Armagh who was hanged in London in 1681 in the aftermath of a so-called "Popish Plot", and canonized in 1975.

Monasterboice

Just north of Drogheda, St Buithe's Abbey at Monasterboice was an early 6th-century foundation. The remains include a round tower with a broken top, and three 9th- or 10th-century high crosses. A masterpiece of the Irish stone carvers, Muireadach's Cross is covered with sculpted panels of Old and New Testament scenes. Beautifully preserved, it is over 5 m (17 ft) tall, with a top carved in the shape of an early church.

Another fine cross to the west is even taller at over 6 m (20 ft), although unlike Muireadach's Cross it isn't a monolith but made of three pieces. It, too, has carved panels of biblical scenes and abstract motifs, but is much more weathered.

Mellifont

In a tranquil valley to the west of Drogheda, Mellifont Abbey was the earliest Cistercian monastery in Ireland, dating from 1142. The main features now are a gatehouse, a fragment of cloister and the pretty lavabo, the monk's washhouse, with five of its eight sides and their round arches still standing.

Boyne Valley

The Boyne is small as Ireland's rivers go, but its significance in her history is unrivalled; the scale of the prehistoric remains suggests that it supported a big population.

The Battle of the Boyne in 1690 was the decisive action of the war which assured the Protestant ascendancy for generations. The two sides met at the river crossing about 6 km (4 miles) west of Drogheda. James II had drawn up his Irish and French forces, some 25,000 strong, on the southern bank. William of Orange's multinational Protestant army of 36,000 occupied the north bank. William himself led the assault on the ford. The fighting was fierce and evenly balanced, but Protestant units then crossed the Boyne to the east and west of the main engagement. To avoid being outflanked, the Jacobite forces retreated; James fled and took ship for France.

Newgrange

A great dome-topped cylindrical mound with a shining white wall (a controversial restoration), the Neolithic passage grave of Newgrange north of the Boyne is more than 80 m (263 ft) wide and up to 10 m (33 ft) high. At its heart is a cruciform burial chamber, reached by a passage 19 m (62 ft) long, the entrance guarded by a huge stone carved with spiral whorls and lozenges. As you squeeze along the corridor you'll make out more designs: swirls, waves and triangles. A special feature is an opening above the tunnel, aligned so that on midwinter's day, December 21, the sun shines directly along it about an hour after sunrise, illuminating the chamber with a golden light.

Around the mound are massive kerbstones carved with the same motifs that you see inside, and a few standing stones survive from a circle that once ringed the mound. A museum and visitor centre near the entrance tell the story of the monuments.

This is one of the most visited sights in Ireland; the restricted access to the chamber means that you have to join a tour. Go early in the day and try to avoid summer weekends.

Knowth

A mound even bigger than Newgrange, Knowth is still being excavated. Two burial chambers have been found, back to back near the middle of the mound, with entrance passages 34 m (114 ft) and 40 m (130 ft) long and so low that it seems unlikely there will ever be public access. About 20 smaller passage tombs cluster close to the big mound, and some of these have been restored. The rock carvings on the kerbstones are the most prolific and varied of their period (about 3000 BC) to be found anywhere.

Kells

The Book of Kells, now in Dublin, put this little town on the map, although only the Irish name of Ceanannas Mór is given on most road signs. Not much is left of the monastery buildings but a high cross in the town centre bears unusual carvings of deer, wrestlers and soldiers with horses. Its top and wheel are broken—it is said to have been used as a gallows during the crushing of the 1798 United Irishmen's revolt.

More Celtic crosses stand in the churchyard at the top of town. The finest, with designs derived from Norse art, stands near an 11th-century round tower, unusual in having five upper windows. So that those who come expecting to see the famous book won't be too disappointed, there's a good facsimile in the church. Across the street, St Columba's House preserves the structure of a 9th-century church of the high-pitched-roof type, like St Kevin's "Kitchen" at Glendalough.

Trim

The massive remains of its early Norman castle, the Augustinian monastery and other ruins dominate the quiet town of Trim. The castle walls, punctuated by semicircular towers, a square keep and main gate are all well preserved, although most of the area inside the walls is green grass.

Across the river is the tall remnant of a tower of the 13th-century St Mary's Abbey. Next to it, the manor house called Talbot's Castle was bought by Jonathan Swift's friend "Stella" in 1717: he may indeed have paid for it. But when he became Dean of St Patrick's, Trim was too far from Dublin for convenient meetings and the house was sold to the Church. Later, as a school, it was attended by the future Duke of Wellington.

Castletown House

West of Dublin, Castletown House at Celbridge is the grandest 18th-century house in Ireland, built in the 1720s for William Connolly, Speaker of the Irish House of Commons. He died in 1729, before it was completed, and his widow, although employing 180 servants, left it in that state. It was only when a great nephew, Tom Connolly, inherited Castletown and married the 15-year-old Lady Louisa Lennox in 1758 that work was renewed.

The classical entrance hall leads to a high staircase hall, with cantilevered stairs set against white baroque plasterwork. The State Bedroom where Speaker Connolly had planned to receive his guests was later used for meetings by Lord Edward Fitzgerald, one of the leaders of the 1798 Rising. The magnificent Long Gallery was decorated in the style of Pompeii after Lady Louisa's visit to Italy in the 1770s.

The Curragh

On the main road west of Dublin, past Newbridge, you'll suddenly emerge into the green expanse of the Curragh, once a training area for the British Army, now for the Irish Army and above all for racehorses. A huge grandstand, silent most of the year, comes alive for the Irish Derby run in May or June.

Howth's picturesque harbour seems light years away from the bustle of Dublin, but it's just a short ride on the DART.

Kildare

The quiet little town of Kildare is transformed whenever there's a race meeting. The cathedral, probably on the site of a convent founded by St Bridget, has been destroyed and rebuilt many times. Its square tower understandably looks like a castle keep.

Irish National Stud

At Tully, close to Kildare, this is a country club for horses. Humans are welcome to visit. From February to June, the big attraction is the foaling unit, where you can look in at the new arrivals, born only a few hours earlier (most births seem to happen between 9 p.m. and 2 a.m.). If you're lucky, you'll see one walking to the paddock when only a day or two old and taking a joyous first gallop, already moving like a racehorse. In the adjoining intensive care unit sick or premature foals can be looked after 24 hours a day. There's often a saddler at work, and a farrier hammering horseshoes or giving one of the residents or visitors some hoof care.

A Horse Museum traces the evolution of the horse and its partnership with humans, in agriculture, transport, warfare and of course racing. Equine genealogies trace the ancestry of famous

31

winners back to one of the three stallions from Arabia or Turkey from whom all racehorses are thought to be descended.

The Japanese Garden next to the Stud, created at the beginning of the 20th century, is one of the best of its kind outside Japan.

Punchestown

The rural racecourse at Punchestown sleeps for most of the year but the April meeting is one of Ireland's big sporting and social events. In a field next to the main gate, a pointed prehistoric standing stone is the tallest in Ireland, 7 m (23 ft) high.

Russborough House

Near Blessington, Russborough is a fine 18th-century Palladian mansion, bought by Sir Alfred Beit (heir to a mining fortune) to house his collection of furniture and art. Some of the most valuable paintings were stolen in 1974 but soon retrieved, only to be taken again in 1986. Most, including a priceless Vermeer, *Lady Writing a Letter*, have since been recovered. You can also see major works by French, Italian and Dutch masters and portraits by Reynolds and Gainsborough.

Sandycove

On the south side of Dublin Bay, Sandycove has become a commuter suburb of Dublin but still feels like the seaside village it was. In 1904, at the invitation of the poet Oliver St John Gogarty, James Joyce was staying in the Martello tower (built during the Napoleonic Wars). He left in a hurry after another guest and his host fired off a gun inside the tower following a night's drinking. He made the tower the setting of the first scene in *Ulysses*, and his publisher Sylvia Beach set it up as a Joyce museum in 1962. The exhibits have grown in number over the years with first editions of his books, the special edition of *Ulysses* illustrated by Matisse, copies of letters between Joyce and Nora Barnacle, his guitar and walking stick, photographs and curios.

Powerscourt

The pretty village of Enniskerry grew up to serve Powerscourt, a great 18th-century house which has been a shell since it was devastated by fire in 1974. The gardens remain, with their grand terraces, balustrades and statuary, borders and lawns. A flight of steps flanked by two superb winged horses stretches down to a lake and fountain, a tamed version of nature contrasted against the wild Wicklow Mountains. The highest waterfall in Ireland is 5 km (3 miles) to the south, reached by a woodland walk or from the road.

THE SOUTHEAST

Southeast Ireland can lay claim to one more hour's sunshine a day than the rest of the island. Interspersed with some of the country's busiest beaches are historic ports and scattered ruins—castles, abbeys and fortresses—that bear witness to the passage of Celts, Vikings, Normans and Anglo-Saxons, who came, conquered and settled. Away from the coast, you can enjoy spectacular scenery, with rugged mountains, fertile valleys and plains and deep lakes.

Wicklow Mountains

Filling the horizon south of Dublin, the Wicklow Mountains are a magnet for walkers. A designated route called the Wicklow Way might take a week or more to walk but you can pick shorter sections: information leaflets are available from Tourist Board offices. For a scenic drive from Dublin, take the road through the Sally Gap or go via Blessington through the Wicklow Gap.

Glendalough

A hidden valley with two lakes, Glendalough was chosen by St Kevin in the 6th century as the site for his monastery. It became rich and famous, and Viking raiders looted it more than once. Wrecked by an army from Dublin in 1398, it went into a decline; the Reformation in the 16th century finished it off.

The visitor centre has good displays and a video, and guided tours start from here. The extensive site is scattered with the ruins of seven churches. Nearest is the roofless cathedral, probably begun in the 9th century. Below it is the older oratory, labelled "St Kevin's Kitchen" because the round belltower looks rather like a chimney. The steep pitched roofs of early churches such as this hide one or more upper rooms above their barrel-vaulted ceilings.

The separate Round Tower, added later, is one of many at Irish monastic sites. They may have been built as places to shelter from attack, perhaps doubling as lookout posts and belfries. Doorways high above the ground support the refuge theory, even if such a chimney-like structure doesn't seem a sensible place to be when raiders are looting and burning.

33

Avondale House

Down the wooded valley of the Avonmore, in a beautiful forest park, Avondale House was the birthplace and home of one of Ireland's heroes, Charles Stewart Parnell. It was opened as a museum in 1991, the centenary of his death. Press cuttings, posters, documents and tributes are on display and a video history is screened. Most moving are his poems to Kitty O'Shea, and their wedding ring which he made from gold mined on the Avondale estate.

Ferns

On the road into Wexford from the north, Ferns was once capital of Leinster and a stronghold of Diarmaid MacMurrough, the man who invited the Normans to Ireland and then conveniently died. The whole town is strewn with ruins, including the keep and chapel of the 13th-century Norman castle.

Enniscorthy

Ireland's rivers were her best roads until modern times, and river ports grew up where ships could get no further upstream and had to unload. The settlement then became the obvious place for a bridge, and a castle for its defence. Enniscorthy on the River Slaney is a perfect example; its four-towered castle is now the county museum. Across the river, the top of Vinegar Hill was the main encampment of the United Irishmen in the 1798 Rising, and the scene of the greatest battle of that campaign, at which the rebels were defeated.

Wexford Town

An almost landlocked harbour near the estuary of the River Slaney was one of the first Viking settlements. The vanguard of the Norman invasions landed not far away at Bannow Bay, and Wexford was the first town they captured.

The long quay is only used by fishing boats and pleasure craft now: the harbour is too shallow for bigger ships. The line of seafront houses is interrupted by the curve of Crescent Quay, centred on a statue of John Barry, a local man who became first commodore of the US Navy. Narrow streets lead up to the town, not much more than one long street with old-world shops and countless pubs and bars. Each October, every room and hall is pressed into service during Wexford's International Opera Festival.

The Irish National Heritage Park, north of Wexford at Ferrycarrig, features replicas of ancient sites, from a Stone Age camp to tombs and a monastic site. Near the entrance, there's a thatched *crannóg* (lake dwelling) and a riverside Viking settlement complete with a Viking longship. A replica Norman motte-and-bailey fort stands on a hilltop, close to a real Norman fortification, probably the first in Ireland, built in 1169.

Johnstown Castle

South of Wexford beyond Murrintown, the 19th-century neo-Gothic Johnstown Castle is set in magnificent gardens and reflected in an ornamental lake. You can wander in the grounds, looking at the walled garden, the hothouses and shrubberies. Fine buildings round the old farmyard house the Irish Agricultural Museum, a collection of farm tools and machinery, country furniture, ingenious domestic inventions and almost anything else to do with rural life.

Rosslare

Holiday homes spread along the coast behind sand dunes and a long beach teeming with birdlife. Ferries from Fishguard, Pembroke, Roscoff and Cherbourg dock just along the coast at Rosslare Harbour.

Waterford City

In the east of the county of the same name, Waterford is some way from the sea but the broad River Suir made it a significant port from Viking times. On the south bank, Reginald's Tower stands on the site of a Viking fort captured by Strongbow's Normans in 1170. Tradition says that he and MacMurrough's daughter Aoife first met here soon after the battle. The masonry at the base looks old enough to be Viking

---

HOME RULER

Charles Stewart Parnell (1846–91) was a Protestant who led the Irish Home Rule Party in the British House of Commons. At the same time, he joined the Land League to fight for the rights of tenant farmers who faced bankruptcy and eviction every time prices fell or crops failed. It developed the tactic of ostracizing unfair landlords and their agents, called the "boycott" after one example. The League's leaders were arrested and Parnell spent several months in Kilmainham Jail. In the 1885 election Parnell's party won almost all the Irish seats, but in 1890 came disaster, the revelation in the divorce court of his adultery with the wife of Captain O'Shea, a former colleague. Parnell refused to stand down as leader, and his party split. When Kitty O'Shea's divorce came through they married, but soon after, on 6 October 1891, he died. His dream of self-government for all Ireland died with him.

work, but the upper parts are Anglo-Norman. After serving as a mint, prison and police station, it's now the Civic Museum.

Along the quay, the Waterford Treasures visitor centre in the Granary has inter-active audio-visual displays of the city's history. When in 1987 a site was cleared for a shopping centre, between Peter, Arundel and High streets, archaeologists were able to excavate part of the Viking settlement; bone implements, jewellery and weapons are on show at the Greyfriars centre.

Waterford's two cathedrals date from the late 18th century. The same Georgian era saw the creation of the elegant Mall and of City Hall, whose chandelier is naturally Waterford glass. The glass factory itself is at Kilbarry, 3 km (2 miles) southwest on the road to Cork. Production started in 1783, but ceased in 1851, when a tax was put on Irish exports by the government in London to stop the factory competing with English manufacturers. The industry was revived in 1947; parts of the factory are open on weekdays for tours.

Kilkenny Town

Ireland's best-preserved medieval city, Kilkenny is a perfect size for exploring on foot, with plenty to see. Orient yourself at the tourist office in Shee's Almshouse (1584) in Rose Inn Street, where the Cityscope Exhibition shows how Kilkenny would have looked in the 1640s, using a scale model and picking out the historic sites with dramatic lighting.

Kilkenny Castle, at the crossing of the River Nore, was owned by the powerful Butler family for over 500 years until they gave it to the state in 1937. On a tour you'll see the long picture gallery, with Butler family portraits by Van Dyck, Kneller and others, and the massive kitchens which are put to use every summer running a restaurant for visitors. Converted stables across the road are the home of the Kilkenny Design Centre, established in the 1960s to improve the quality of craft products: glass, ceramics, fabrics, knitwear and jewellery.

Dunmore Cave

About 11 km (7 miles) north of Kilkenny are a series of caves which have been known for at least a thousand years. Ancient records tell of a massacre by the Vikings of people who had taken refuge inside, and modern excavations certainly turned up human bones from that time, as well as Viking jewellery and coins.

*The Rock of Cashel (top);
16th-century stone carving at
Jerpoint Abbey (bottom).*

Jerpoint Abbey

The Cistercian abbey of Jerpoint, near Thomastown, is full of wonderful details. The best way to make sure of seeing them all is to buy the visitor's guide leaflet at the entrance.

Beneath the tower is the tomb of the first abbot, Felix O'Dullany, who died in 1202; a worn effigy shows him holding a crozier with a serpent biting its end. Later tombs have fine sculptures of apostles, saints and archangels, carved by the local O'Tunney family in the early 16th century. A strange life-size picture cut in stone depicts two knights, called "The Brothers", perhaps crusaders or Templars. The partly restored cloisters include many vignettes in stone: look for the frowning 14th-century knight, the lady in a pleated dress and little figures of imps and devils.

Kells

West of Jerpoint along a narrow country lane you'll suddenly come upon a surreal sight. Amid grazing sheep, grey stone towers and massive walls big enough for a whole city guard the ruined priory of Kells (not the one after which the Book is named). The lonely splendour of the setting and the amazing preservation of the defences make it well worth a detour.

Carrick-on-Suir

Henry VIII's second wife Anne Boleyn (1507–36) is said to have been born in one of the 15th-century towers of Ormond Castle. The adjoining Tudor mansion was added some years after Anne lost her head. Because there was still a need for fortification in most of Ireland, houses in this style, with its array of stone-mullioned windows and pointed gables, are extremely rare. The Elizabethan long gallery is unique in Ireland.

Cashel

The Rock of Cashel stands 80 m (260 ft) above the plain, so it was a natural site for a fortress. Crowned with ancient and sacred buildings, it's one of Ireland's most visited places. To avoid crowds, time your visit for early morning or evening (it stays open until 7.30 p.m. in summer).

A worn 11th-century high cross depicting Christ and a figure presumed to be St Patrick can be seen in the 15th-century Hall of the Vicars Choral, adjoining the entrance. According to legend, St Patrick said one of his first masses in Ireland here, and on a later visit in 450 he is reported to have converted Aengus, King of Munster.

The Irish-Romanesque Cormac's Chapel, consecrated in 1134, may appear to have been built at an odd angle into the southeast corner of the much larger cathedral. In fact, the chapel is at least a century older, and it's the *cathedral* which was added, aligned east-west as had become the norm by then. Inside, a 12th-century sarcophagus, possibly Cormac's own, is decorated with carvings of entwined snakes in the Scandinavian Urnes style.

The 13th-century cathedral is the biggest building on the Rock; the fortress-like appearance dates from the 15th century when an archbishop added a castle to the west end of the nave.

At the foot of the Rock, the Brú Ború Heritage Centre stages traditional music and dance performances in summer. Off the town's one main street, the elegant 18th-century bishops' palace is now a hotel.

Cahir

The little market town is dominated by its 14th-century castle, on a rocky island in the Suir. Now thoroughly restored, it's sometimes used as a film set. You can tour on your own or wait for the guides to explain the details: the castle is a textbook of medieval military architecture.

The 1817 Protestant church is credited to John Nash, and a unique house called Swiss Cottage may also have been designed by him. South of the town in the castle grounds, it's a thatched retreat built for Lord Cahir so he and his wife could get away from the formality of the castle and play at being happy rustics.

From Cahir to the south coast, the most direct route is also the most scenic. Called the Vee, after a particularly extreme bend, it zigzags through the heather and over the ridge of the Knockmealdown Mountains by way of a pass called the Gap. On a clear day, stop near the top for the views or a walk—a favourite Sunday outing for local people.

Dungarvan

Deep-sea fishing boats and pleasure craft use the big harbour at Dungarvan. To the south of the port is a pocket of the Gaeltacht (the Irish-speaking community) called Ring *(An Rinn)*, an area of scattered cottages and farms, but with its own radio station. If you're driving, locate it on your car radio and hear some traditional music, even if you can't follow the talk.

The little resort of Ardmore was the site of St Declan's monastery, notable now for its sturdy little 11th-century Romanesque cathedral. Boldly sculpted but worn carvings below the west window show Adam and Eve, the Judgement of Solomon, the Adoration of the Magi and the Last Judgement.

THE SOUTHWEST

Youghal, Cork City, Cobh, Kinsale, Clonakilty, Bantry, Castletownbere, Killarney, Ring of Kerry, Dingle Peninsula, Tralee

From the rich farmlands of County Cork in the east to the rocks and bogs of Kerry, the southwest corner of Ireland combines superb scenery and an eventful history. Among many highlights are Kinsale, Killarney, the Ring of Kerry and the Dingle Peninsula.

Youghal

On the west bank of the Blackwater estuary, the little port of Youghal (say "yawl") used to be known for its lace. In the town centre, the four-storey Clock House, built in the 1770s, houses a local museum. Near some fine restored almshouses dated 1610, Church Street leads to St Mary's Church, with a separate belfry and 13th-century tower. The interior is crowded with tombs and carvings, notably the full-colour monument to Richard Boyle, the "Great Earl of Cork", which he designed himself in about 1620. Effigies of his two wives, praying, and nine of his children surround the reclining figure of the earl in his armour and robes.

Slea Head Drive on Dingle Peninsula is one of the most scenic in County Kerry.

Elizabeth I awarded land in the area to Sir Walter Raleigh, and legend claims that he brought the potato to Ireland and planted the first crop. There's no evidence for the story, though he certainly visited Youghal several times.

Cork City

The Republic's second city grew up on low-lying islands in the River Lee, and some of its streets once carried water traffic. Grand Parade was an arm of the river until it was covered over in the 18th century, and other waterways still criss-cross the centre.

Cork probably started with St Finbarr's monastery in the 6th century. By the 18th century it was a prosperous trading and manufacturing centre, the focus of a rich agricultural region. In the 1919–21 troubles, the city suffered at the hands of the Black and Tans, who murdered the Nationalist lord mayor, Thomas MacCurtain. It took the boom of the 1970s to get things moving again with the growth of light industry and the service sector, and Cork today is brimming with life.

The best way to see the sights is to walk; the tourist office at the 41 south end of Grand Parade has maps. Don't miss the restored English Market, leading off Grand Parade; then you might follow St Patrick Street to Cork's popular meeting point, the statue of Father Theobald Mathew, 19th-century temperance campaigner. Along Lavitt's Quay, the Opera House is a modern venue for touring productions and theatre—the Cork Theatre Company specializes in the Irish dramatists.

On a steep hill across the river from the Opera House, Shandon is one of the oldest parts of the city: St Ann's Church (1722), with its curious steeple, salmon weathervane and famous bells, is a landmark.

Over the southern arm of the Lee from Grand Parade, Red Abbey is one of the few medieval relics, surviving from an Augustinian monastery. For a view of Cork and its superb harbour, take to the water on an excursion or go by boat to Cobh (see below).

Blarney Castle

An imposing 15th-century tower house, 8 km (5 miles) northwest of Cork City, Blarney is a former seat of the MacCarthys. Elizabeth I of England complained of the sweet-talking MacCarthy, Lord of Blarney at the time: "This is all Blarney: what he says he never does!" The legend that those who kiss the Blarney Stone will have the same gift of fluency is probably a 19th-century invention, but up on the battlements the tourists lie back and bend their necks until their lips touch the right stone.

Jameson Heritage Centre

At Midleton, 21 km (15 miles) east of Cork City, the centre tells the story of Irish whiskey in the beautifully restored distillery where it was made from 1825 to 1975. There's an audio-visual show, a tour, and a chance to sample five Irish brands plus a Scotch and an American bourbon for comparison. The guides relate the facts and the fairy stories so well that you'll hardly notice that you don't see any actual production. That happens in the new buildings nearby.

Cobh

On the long inlet between Cork and the sea, the port of Cobh (meaning "cove" and pronounced that way) has seen its share of tragedy and glamour. Known as Queenstown until 1921, it grew in importance when ships became too big to reach Cork itself.

Convicts were first shipped to Australia from here in 1791; troopships embarked soldiers for the Napoleonic, Crimean and Boer wars and emigrants left from Cobh until well into the 20th century. It was the last port of call of the *Titanic* in 1912, and when the *Lusitania* was sunk by a German submarine in 1915 the survivors were brought here.

The restored Victorian railway station on the quay houses an exhibition called The Queenstown Story, using models, paintings, old photographs, newsreels and dramatic sound effects. Of the 187 passengers who joined the *Titanic* here, most were poor emigrants travelling steerage, and almost all were drowned. Happier pictures evoke the days of the transatlantic liners in the 1920s and 30s when film stars and royalty came ashore for a tour or a civic reception.

Above all, the exhibition tells the story of the 3 million Irish who sailed from this quayside to seek a better life. From a few thousand in the 1830s, emigration jumped to 239,000 in the famine years of the 1840s, and peaked at 390,000 in the 1880s. In the early days, cooped up in unseaworthy "coffin ships", ill when they boarded and seasick from the moment they sailed, many died on the voyage. Outside the station, a statue depicts a woman and her two children—a particular family, but the memorial honours all the emigrants.

Kinsale

A sheltered little fishing port south of Cork City, Kinsale has become a yachting and holiday centre, with picturesque old shops and some good restaurants.

It has an eventful past. A Spanish expedition landed in 1601 to aid an Irish rising against the English, only to be besieged for ten weeks by English troops. Irish forces failed to relieve the Spaniards and they were forced to surrender, precipitating the Flight of the Earls. James II came ashore at Kinsale in 1689 to try to regain his throne, and left again from here in 1690 after the Battle of the Boyne.

Guarding the west side of the harbour, star-shaped James Fort was built after the 1601 Spanish invasion to deter any similar threat. Charles Fort on the eastern side dates from the 1670s, and housed British troops right up to 1921. Some of the buildings are off-limits because of their dangerous state.

Back in the town centre, the church of St Multose is partly Norman. Desmond Castle is a 16th-century tower house where French prisoners were held during the Napoleonic Wars. The old town hall houses a small museum —notice the old list of tolls and duties payable by market traders and importers in the entrance.

Take the road south towards the Old Head of Kinsale and then walk to the tip of the peninsula for spectacular clifftop views.

43

Clonakilty

A quiet little west Cork town, Clonakilty comes alive during its summer music festival. The nearby hamlet of Woodfield was the birthplace of the Irish Free State leader Michael Collins in 1890, and he was killed not far from here, near Crookstown, during the Civil War in 1922.

Baltimore

The tiny port of Baltimore is almost deserted for most of the year, but in summer its narrow streets can be choked with traffic. Opposite a ruined fort, a pub called the Algiers Inn recalls the year 1631, when Barbary pirates all the way from the Mediterranean carried off over a hundred of the villagers into slavery.

Bantry

Bantry Bay is the biggest deepwater inlet in Ireland, but facing southwest, it fails to give much shelter from the prevailing winds. The town of Bantry can serve as a base for touring the coast and mountains.

Bantry House, built in the 18th and 19th century, is still lived in by the White family who have owned it since 1739. Now they run part of it as a hotel. The dining room is a riot of blue and gold, under the gaze of enormous portraits of George III and Queen Charlotte by Ramsay. Outside in the Italianate gardens, climb the flights of steps for a view of the house and bay.

In the stable block, the French Armada Exhibition records a failed French invasion attempt in 1796. A 1:6 scale model of the frigate *La Surveillante* is on display, with cannon and other objects recovered from the wreck of the ship, found under the waters of the bay in 1985.

From Ballylickey at the head of the bay, the scenery along the inland road over the Keimaneigh Pass towards Macroom is dramatic. Lough Gougane Barra, the Holy Lake, is surrounded on three sides by precipitous rocks and tumbling waterfalls.

Glengarriff

At the head of an inlet off Bantry Bay, Glengarriff is hemmed in by odd-shaped mountains and rocks. It became a genteel resort in the 19th century; palm trees tell you how warm and sheltered it is. Offshore, Garinish Island is laid out as an Italian garden.

Castletownbere

On the quiet shores of the Beara (or Bere) Peninsula, this fishing port comes as a surprise. You can hear Spanish, Portuguese, French and Russian spoken in the town, and even see Russian women doing their shopping when their fishing fleets are in the harbour.

Colourful Kinsale has gained quite a reputation in gourmet circles.

Killarney

Set amid beautiful lake and mountain scenery, Killarney has been in the tourism business since the mid-19th century. Souvenir shops, restaurants and pubs line Main Street and its extension, High Street. The National Museum of Irish Transport in the town centre holds treasures such as a 1904 Belgian Germain and a magnificent Mercedes 540K of 1938, plus penny-farthing bicycles and baby carriages. Other diversions include horse racing and Gaelic football, the local favourite spectator sport. At weekends some pubs and bars put on traditional music nights.

But the main point of visiting Killarney is to get out of it. Horse-drawn "jaunting cars" wait at vantage points; if you'd like to ride in one, ask the driver (the jarvey) where he can take you, how long the trip will be and the price.

Of the famous lakes, Lough Leane (or Lower Lake) is closest to town; glass-topped waterbuses can take you on a tour. The ruined Ross Castle by the shore held out for months against Cromwellian forces, until their commander heard a legend that it would only fall if ships ever sailed on the lake. He had some hauled up from Kenmare, and the fortress duly surrendered.

45

The Franciscan Muckross Abbey, south of town, was wrecked by Cromwell's troops in 1652. Muckross House nearby was built in 1843 in Elizabethan style, and given by its owners to the Irish state in 1932. You can stroll in the lovely gardens, but there's a lot to see in the house as well. The basements house craft workshops and displays, while the Kerry Country Life Experience in the grounds is a real working farm, reviving methods used before mechanization.

Gap of Dunloe

West of the lakes, a gorge through the mountains, 6 km (4 miles) long, is one of the "musts" of a visit to Killarney. Starting at Kate Kearney's Cottage, you can ride part of the way by horse or pony, or take a jaunting car, cycle, or just walk—at a steady pace it will take you about three hours to the head of the gap and back. Some tours by minibus link up with a boat trip on the Upper Lake and downriver to Lough Leane.

MacGillycuddy's Reeks are the memorably named mountains to the south and west of Killarney, sliced through by the Gap of Dunloe. Carrantuohill, the highest peak in Ireland at 1,041 m (3,416 ft), can be a fairly easy day's hill walk, rather than a serious climb. Even better views can be had from Mangerton, 840 m (2,756 ft), standing apart from the Reeks due south of Killarney.

Ring of Kerry

Talk about the Iveragh Peninsula and you may get a blank look, but most people have heard of the Ring of Kerry, the 175-km (108-mile) route that links the varied sights around this scenic coast. Here, we have chosen the clockwise direction.

Kenmare, a convenient starting point, is a centre for walking and fishing, with some good hotels and a fine golf course. A gentle coastline brings you to Parknasilla, a quiet resort where seals may be seen offshore. Sneem, backed by the Caha Mountains, has brightly painted houses around a village green. At Castlecove, look for the sign to Staigue Fort, 4 km (2.5 miles) inland, a remarkable prehistoric ring-fort, with stone walls up to 4 m (13 ft) high, terraced internally and with two small chambers in the walls. It may date from about 500 BC but would have been in use for centuries and often repaired.

Near Caherdaniel, a loop off the main road down to the sea leads to Derrynane House, the home of Daniel O'Connell, the campaigner for Catholic rights who lived here on and off until 1847. It was sadly neglected after the last of the family died, and some of O'Connell's books and possessions were lost, but many survived and more have been donated.

Waterville is an old-established resort with a choice of accommodation. Standing stones and dolmens show the area was an important ancient burial site.

At Portmagee you can cross a bridge to Valentia Island, starting point for the first Atlantic cable in 1866, opening telegraphic communication with America. Slate quarries on its north coast provided roofs for the Paris Opera, the Houses of Parliament in London and countless billiard tables.

The Skelligs

Just over the Valentia Bridge, the Skellig Experience tells of the life of the early Irish Christians in monasteries such as Skellig Michael, one of a group of rocky islets off the coast. A modern cruise boat leaves from the quay to circle the Skelligs, but other boats give you some time ashore on Skellig Michael, a forbidding pinnacle of rock 10 km (6 miles) offshore. From the little landing stage, steep steps climb to the site of the monastery, which survived here on and off from the 7th to the 12th century. Nearer the coast, the islet of Little Skellig is a bird sanctuary, a major breeding ground for gannets; landings are not permitted.

Killorglin

August brings crowds from near and far to Killorglin's Puck Fair. The star of the show, crowned king for the day, is a handsome billy-goat, on top of a stand in the town centre, a custom which may date from pagan times.

Dingle Peninsula

Pointing due west, the scenic Dingle Peninsula is peppered with prehistoric and early Christian remains. The tip is a mainly Gaelic-speaking area, with road signs to match.

Dingle

Claiming to be the most westerly town in Europe, Dingle *(An Daingean)* doubles its population in summer as visitors crowd its restaurants and pack its pubs on music nights. The streets are lined with terraced houses and shops, painted in rainbow colours, and the sheltered harbour hosts trawlers from all over Europe.

Dunbeg

An Iron Age fort on a cliff edge near the road, protected by multiple banks and ditches, Dunbeg has a complex entrance and an underground passage which may have been part of an escape route. Radio-carbon tests suggest the site was fortified about 580 BC and was in use until the 11th century AD.

Along the road near Fahan, prehistoric stone "beehive" huts are scattered over the slopes of Mount Eagle, 517 m (1,696 ft) high and worth a climb; on clear days the views are superb. At Slea Head, a sandy cove entices hardy souls to swim on the rare calm days. Offshore, the rugged Blaskett Islands lie deserted since the last inhabitants left in 1953. In summer, boats sail to Great Blaskett from Dingle and Dunquin.

West of Smerwick Harbour on the north coast of the peninsula, hidden among reeds, are traces of Fort del Oro, built in 1579 by a Spanish expedition. It was sent to support a Catholic rebellion during the reign of Elizabeth I, but the fort was cut off by the English Navy and the defenders slaughtered. A modern stone monument pays tribute to the dead.

East of Ballyferriter is the little stone church called the Gallarus Oratory. Shaped like an upturned boat, blunt at both ends, it probably dates from the 8th century.

Mount Brandon, at 953 m (3,127 ft) the second-highest peak in Ireland, fills the horizon to the east. From Ballybrack, Saint's Road climbs to the summit and the ruins of St Brendan's Oratory. The mountain meets the sea so suddenly at the north coast that there's no room for a road, so cars have to return via Dingle town and the scenic Conor Pass.

Tralee

Famous in song, Tralee is no beauty spot but nevertheless hosts the August "Rose of Tralee" beauty contest (for anyone with a hint of Irish ancestry), with a full week of parades, horse races and a street carnival. The National Folklore Theatre stages Irish music and dance, and Kerry the Kingdom is a three-stage exhibition and "ride"; a video show extols the landscape and culture of the county.

South of the town, the restored Blennerville Windmill still grinds wheat for flour 200 years after it was built. At the nearby quay where many left Ireland for ever, an Emigration Exhibition tells their story. A full-size replica of the sailing ship *Jeanie Johnston* which carried some of them was built here in 1999 for a commemorative voyage to North America.

Ardfert

Northwest of Tralee, the long grey ruin of Ardfert Cathedral stands on the probable site of the church of St Brendan ("the Navigator"). Near here on Good Friday 1916, a German submarine put the Irish nationalist Sir Roger Casement ashore. His intention seems to have been not to join the planned Easter Rising but to try to postpone it. In any event, he was soon arrested, convicted of treason and executed.

THE WEST

Limerick City and Surroundings, County Clare, Aran Islands, Galway City, Clonmacnois, Clonfert, Connemara

From the stony wonderland of the Burren to friendly Galway City, the wilds of Connemara and the mystical Aran Islands, the west has enough attractions to keep visitors busy for a month. Many of them arrive at Shannon Airport near Limerick, the crossroads of west and southwest Ireland.

Limerick City and Surroundings

A Viking settlement on an island near the mouth of the River Shannon, Limerick was taken over by the Normans and strengthened by the building of King John's Castle, whose walls reflect in the river next to Thomond Bridge. Bridge Street crosses the narrower Abbey River to Irish Town. O'Connell Street, Limerick's main thoroughfare, still has vestiges of 18th-century Georgian elegance; some of the terrace houses rival Dublin's best, while others have fallen into disrepair.

In about 1200, determined to bring his Norman and Gaelic lords to heel, King John ordered the construction of the biggest fortress yet seen in the west of Ireland. Its greatest tests came in four terrible sieges more than 400 years later. In 1642, Irish forces took it, using cannon mounted on

the tower of St Mary's Cathedral. It held out for six months in 1651 before it fell to Cromwell's son-in-law Henry Ireton, who died of the plague just ten days later.

After the Battle of the Boyne in 1690, William of Orange's forces threatened Limerick, until the Irish cavalry commander Patrick Sarsfield led a surprise attack on their supply column and destroyed it. The following year, Limerick was again besieged. After appalling losses, surrender terms were agreed, giving the defenders the choice of joining William's army or going abroad. Almost all went to France, some of the "Wild Geese" who fought in half the armies of Europe for the next century and more.

The castle has been well restored, and a colourful exhibition and video tell the story of the city from Viking times to the present. Walkways over the castle's foundations reveal the remains of pre-Norman houses discovered in recent excavations.

Protestant St Mary's Cathedral was begun in 1172, and has been frequently rebuilt since; the Romanesque doorway is probably the only original part. Inside, the 15th-century choirstalls are a rarity in Ireland.

The Hunt Museum in the elegant 1769 Custom House has fine Bronze Age jewellery and weapons, early Christian metal work, Irish and European silver, a bronze horse by Leonardo da Vinci and paintings by Renoir, Picasso and Jack B. Yeats.

Adare

A picturebook village of thatched cottages, 16 km (10 miles) southwest of Limerick, Adare was just a collection of poor huts and hovels until the 2nd Earl of Dunraven transformed it in the 1820s. Having rehoused the villagers, he restored one ruined abbey as the Catholic church and another to be his family's mausoleum. He turned the family house, Adare Manor, into a magnificent Elizabethan-style mansion. It's now a luxury hotel, but you can make arrangements to see inside. Every July, Adare holds a music festival with international orchestras and soloists.

Lough Gur

This small lake south of Limerick seems to have been sacred to a succession of past civilizations, judging from the treasures it has yielded up. Excavations around it have revealed Neolithic graves and house foundations from 2500 to 2000 BC. The Grange stone circle, 60 m (200 ft) in diameter and dating from about 2100 BC is one of the biggest in Ireland, with 113 stones—almost the full complement—still in place.

Bruree

Eamon de Valera, who dominated Irish politics for 60 years, was born in New York in 1882, but he was sent back to Ireland when only two, on the death of his father. He attended the village school at Bruree, south of Limerick. A leader of the 1916 Rising, founder of the Fianna Fáil, several times prime minister and then president, he returned to the village at the age of 90 to open the de Valera Museum in his old school.

Bunratty Castle

A massive 15th-century rectangular keep, Bunratty was restored in the 1950s and 60s; its great halls and other rooms are furnished with pieces from the 14th to the 17th centuries. Medieval-style banquets are staged nightly for tour groups, with entertainment including folk music and dances.

Bunratty Folk Park is a village of replica and original buildings from all over the west of Ireland. In summer a *céilí*, or traditional

Thatched cottages, like this one in Connemara, are fast disappearing from the Irish landscape.

Irish evening celebration, is held nightly in the great barn.

Shannon Airport

As the most westerly airfield in Europe, Shannon became important after World War II, refuelling transatlantic airliners which had taken over the service from the flying boats based at Foynes. Later, when they could fly from New York to London or Paris non-stop, Shannon invented the duty-free shop and offered low-cost fuel to attract them. It remains a main entry point for North American visitors.

Foynes

From 1939 until 1945, North Atlantic passenger flights took off or landed at Foynes. The service was operated by flying boats, their "runway" the waters of the Shannon estuary. The old terminal is now the Flying Boat Museum, with memorabilia and historic film clips.

Craggaunowen Project

On a side road west of Quin, replicas of ancient buildings including a *crannóg* (lake dwelling) are set in the grounds of a 16th-century tower house. A section of a *togher*, or wooden track across a bog, is not a replica but part of an Iron Age original, and a 3,500-year-old dugout canoe is another extraordinary survival.

On display in the tower is the *Brendan*, a hide-covered boat which was sailed across the Atlantic in 1976, to show that the legend of St Brendan's voyage might be true. Depending on how you interpret the 9th-century manuscript telling of the monk's adventures, he may have reached America in about 565, perhaps by way of Iceland, Greenland and Newfoundland.

CRUISING THE SHANNON

It's a different way to see Ireland, from a comfortable cruiser on her longest river, 260 km (161 miles) from source to sea. Sometimes you'll be far from shore in the broad expanse of a lough. Then the low green banks close in, from time to time revealing the ruin of an ancient abbey. You can tie up and go ashore to see the sights, go to a pub or spend the night. Only half a dozen locks interrupt the flow, and between the main cruise bases at Killaloe and Portumna, there are none at all. The options include four-, six- and eight-berth boats and you can pick them up and leave them at different points. A more luxurious way is on a 12-passenger hotel barge, with meals, drinks and shore excursions included.

Killaloe

At the southern end of Lough Derg, Killaloe, with its 13-arch stone bridge, is the starting point for many Shannon cruises. In its 12th-century St Flannan's Cathedral, the Thorgrim stone is part of an ancient high cross, uniquely marked with both ogham script and Viking runes. St Flannan's Oratory nearby has the barrel-vaulted ceiling and steep roof typical of early Irish churches.

The 130 sq km (50 sq miles) of Lough Derg make it the biggest of the Shannon lakes and a favourite of birdwatchers and anglers. Holy Island in Scarriff Bay is covered with monastic ruins from the 6th to the 17th centuries including high crosses and a capless round tower.

County Clare

Clare was in the vanguard of agitation for Irish rights and independence, supporting the Land League in the 1880s and electing Daniel O'Connell in 1828. For over 40 years Eamon de Valera was MP for East Clare. Tourism and European Union funds have brought an astonishing amount of new building—you'll scarcely see an old thatched cottage now.

Cliffs of Moher

The Irish coast outdoes itself here with cliffs up to 200 m (660 ft) high. Thousands of seabirds nest in the crevices and their cries compete with the ceaseless wind and roaring sea. Crowds gather on summer days but even a short walk will leave them behind. O'Brien's Tower was erected in 1835 by an eccentric landlord Cornelius O'Brien, who also put up the fences of great stone slabs.

The Burren

Northwest Clare is an austere plateau of bare limestone, deeply fissured by the action of rainwater. Called the Burren from *boireann*, "rocky land", it's a perfect example of what geologists call karst landscape. Hundreds of stone forts, tombs and networks of walls are scattered over it.

At first sight the Burren seems as infertile as a desert, but look

TWO GEOLOGICAL WONDERS OF THE WORLD
The close-packed hexagonal columns of the **Giant's Causeway** on the north coast, and the great expanses of limestone pavement of the **Burren** in the west are uncannily regular, but entirely natural.

closely and you'll find a profusion of plants growing in sheltered cracks. Tiny thorn bushes like bonsais hug the rock, folded round its contours by the wind. Come in May and June to see the brilliant blue gentians, creamy mountain avens, little rock roses and 23 varieties of orchids. At any time of year, the area is a natural rock garden, with plants that usually prefer alpine or Mediterranean climates.

At Kilfenora, the Burren Centre features the geology, plants, wildlife and archaeology of the region. Nearby to the northeast, Ballykinvarga is the most impressive of the Burren's Iron Age rock forts. East of Kilfenora, the road towards Ballyvaughan passes through fine examples of limestone "pavement", as flat as an airfield but slashed by deep chasms. Look for signs to Poulnabrone, a great dolmen topped by a huge flat stone; it dates from around 3300 BC.

Doolin

The fishing village of Doolin is known for its folk music scene, centred on the pubs which are jammed all summer long. Offshore, the low outlines of the Aran Islands hover like a mirage in the mist; a ferry service operates in summer.

To the north, between Fanore and Black Head, the Burren descends in terraces to the sea. Somehow the local cows find enough to eat among the rocks.

Ballyvaughan

A fishing village which has turned to tourism, Ballyvaughan has several restaurants and hotels. Inland, the commercial Aillwee Cave was an underground river channel until the end of the last Ice Age, so stalactites and stalagmites have had little time to grow. More interesting are the hollows that were scraped out long ago by brown bears who moved in to hibernate.

Aran Islands

Three low limestone outcrops off the coast in Galway Bay, the Aran Islands are actually a geological extension of the Burren. Tiny in size and population, they preserved ways of life which were vanishing from the rest of Ireland. Now they are changing too; flights arrive daily, weather permitting, and ferries disgorge crowds of summer visitors.

Inishmore

The name, *Inis Mór* in Gaelic, means "the Big Island". With a length of 15 km (9 miles), this is by far the largest of the three. The ferries dock at Kilronan, where bicycles can be hired. The less active can take a pony-trap or minibus tour.

The much-loved national animal of Ireland is the horse, raised on sweet and plentiful grass.

The villages are on the north coast, where lanes meander between stone walls enclosing little fields of pasture or potatoes. Most of them were once bare rock: the soil was built up from layers of seaweed and sand. At Kilmurvy, 7 km (4 miles) west of Kilronan, a track leads to the south coast and the prehistoric fortress of Dún Aengus. Perched on a 90-m (300-ft) vertical cliff, its massive semicircular walls end only at the very edge of the precipice. It is presumed to date from the Iron Age, perhaps 100 BC, and may once have been circular—the rest having dropped into the sea in cliff falls. (Other Iron Age forts,

Dún Eoghanachta to the north-west and Dún Eochla at the island's highest point *are* circular.)

Inishmore is dotted with the ruins of monastic sites and old churches: the 12th-century St Ciaran's Monastery is just off the coast road west of Kilronan. West of Kilmurvy, the so-called Seven Churches amount to scattered ruins and the restored church of St Brecan. Back at Kilronan, the Aran Heritage Centre has superb photographs and displays on the history and culture of the islands.

Inishmaan

Less than 5 km (3 miles) long, the middle island *(Inis Meáin)* gets 55 far fewer visitors than the others, and life seems to have changed less. Men still go fishing, off the shore, from small craft or out on the handful of bigger boats. The main prehistoric sites are the oval Dún Conor fort on the central ridge and a Bronze Age tomb. During the Celtic revival at the end of the 19th-century, the writer John Millington Synge spent several summers here. His book, *The Aran Islands*, and the photographs he took made a unique record of island life.

Inisheer

The smallest of the three and nearest to the mainland, Inisheer *(Inis Oírr)* is low and flat, apart from a rocky outcrop topped by the irregular Creggankeel ring fort re-used in the 15th century as the outer wall of O'Brien's Castle.

Galway City

The site, between the River Corrib and Galway Bay, was fortified by the Normans, with massive city walls to keep out the fierce Gaelic tribes. Thus protected, Galway's merchants flourished. Restrictions on Irish trade in the 19th century hit Galway hard, and famine made matters worse. The depression began to lift in the 1960s and now the city is as cheerful as you could wish.

On the corner of Shop Street and Abbeygate Street, Lynch's Castle is the best preserved of the townhouses built by prosperous traders. Dating from around 1600, the four-storey house with its elaborate stonework now serves as a bank. Just off Shop Street, the Church of St Nicholas is the largest medieval church in Ireland, dating from about 1320. Inside is the striking Lynch Tomb with its flame-like stone tracery (the flamboyant style found on many 15th- and 16th-century tombs in Ireland).

Narrow High Street and Quay Street lead to a section of old city wall known as the Spanish Arch, adjoined by the local museum. Upstream, an old salmon weir

THREE ROMANTIC RUINS FROM THE AGE OF THE SAINTS Glendalough south of Dublin was founded by St Kevin; the fortress-like cluster of churches and palaces on the **Rock of Cashel** in Tipperary was often visited by St Patrick; and St Ciaran established **Clonmacnois** beside the River Shannon.

gave its name to a bridge over the Corrib; in a good year plenty of salmon still make their way up-river to spawn. Wolfe Tone Bridge leads to the Claddagh ("the Beach"), formerly a Gaelic-speaking fishing village which gave its name to the Claddagh ring design of hands clasped around a crowned heart.

Coole Park

Southeast of Galway City, near Gort, Coole Park was the home of Lady Gregory, playwright and life-long friend of W. B. Yeats. He was a frequent visitor, first coming here to convalesce in 1898. The house was demolished in 1941, but the gardens are now a public park. Literary pilgrims come to see a great copper beech initialled by Yeats, his brother Jack, Shaw with an elaborate GBS, Sean O'Casey and more.

Thoor Ballylee, down a lane to the east, is a 16th-century tower which Yeats bought in 1916, and where he was living when he was elected a senator of the new Irish Free State in 1922 and when he was awarded the Nobel Prize for Literature the following year. The shop has a comprehensive stock of books, almost anything related to Irish writing.

Ballinasloe

Respectable-looking Ballinasloe takes on a different character in October, the time of the sheep and horse fair, an ancient gathering of dealers, gypsies and tinkers from all over Ireland. The most famous sale ever made here was that of Napoleon's horse Marengo, after Waterloo. By the 1860s, 4,000 horses and 100,000 sheep were changing hands during the week of the fair. People said the roads were so jammed with livestock they had to walk from the station to the town on the sheeps' backs! Nowadays, the fair has become a big agricultural show with all sorts of fringe activities.

Clonmacnois

In a tranquil setting on the banks of the Shannon, Clonmacnois was one of Ireland's most important monasteries. Founded in about 545 by St Ciaran, it was often sacked by the Vikings, then by Irish enemies, and finally destroyed in 1552 during the Reformation.

The ruins include two round towers: O'Rourke's Tower near the landing stage and MacCarthy's Tower by the northern boundary, unusually with its entrance at ground level. According to monastic records it dates from 1124. The cathedral, near the entrance, was started in the 10th century, but the striking north doorway topped by a statue of St Patrick dates from the 14th century. Opposite the west door, the

tall, eroded Cross of the Scriptures is carved with scenes from the life of Christ and the Last Judgement on the west face and the foundation of Clonmacnois by St Ciaran on the east face. The tiny 10th-century church where Ciaran is said to be buried stands in the middle of the site.

Clonfert

Few such small villages can boast a cathedral. Clonfert's, dedicated to St Brendan, dates from about 1200, and its Romanesque doorway is one of the sights of Ireland. Six concentric arches stand on inward-sloping columns, their capitals carved into pagan-looking animal heads, all surmounted by an intricate tall gable.

Connemara

What now looks so picturesque was once the scene of great suffering, as too many people tried to subsist by growing crops on the poorest of soils. Almost all the land was either mountain or bog. Coming from Galway City, the main road picks a narrow path between the two. On the left is a wild waste of peat, swamp and a thousand little lakes. On the right are the Maumturk Mountains and then the cluster of peaks known

Abandoned to the elements, the stony ruins of Clonmacnois.

as the Twelve Bens (or "Pins") of Connemara; the highest being Benbuan at 730 m (2,395 ft). Maps and route guide booklets are available from Tourist Board offices, and from the Connemara National Park visitor centre near Letterfrack, where you can learn about the flora, fauna and sights.

Clifden

A quiet spot that comes alive in summer, Clifden has several good restaurants where you may find local salmon, lobsters, oysters and mussels. About 6 km (4 miles) south of the town a wing-shaped stone monument honours John Alcock and Arthur Whitten Brown, who crash-landed their Vickers Vimy in the great bog after making the first non-stop transatlantic flight in 1919.

Killary Harbour

A deep, narrow inlet winds nearly 15 km (10 miles) inland between the mountains. Killary's lower slopes are etched with traces of long-abandoned potato fields. Today the crop is shellfish, grown on frames in the sheltered water. Near the head of the inlet, the Leenane Cultural Centre puts on occasional demonstrations of sheep-shearing, spinning and weaving. Sheep, including some old and rare breeds, graze in the fields, and in season you may be invited to feed a pet lamb.

THE NORTHWEST

County Mayo, Killala, Knock, County Sligo,
County Donegal, Inishowen Peninsula

The counties of Mayo and Donegal are as wild and remote as anywhere in Ireland. Huge cliffs alternate with lonely beaches washed by the cleanest waters in Europe. Whether fishing in the sea or the rivers, hill walking or riding on horseback or bicycle, there's no end to the outdoor activities on offer. Literary pilgrims come to the gentler landscapes of Sligo, in the footsteps of Nobel Prize-winning poet W. B. Yeats.

County Mayo

The main road into Mayo from the south heads for Westport up the valley of the Erriff, famous for salmon fishing. An even more beautiful route follows the north side of Killary Harbour, then cuts through the mountains along the Bundorragha river. Passing Doo Lough, hemmed in by mountains, the road meets the coast again at Louisburgh, a town of neat houses and holiday cottages.

Croagh Patrick

The peak of Croagh Patrick, at 765 m (2,510 ft), looks almost conical, like a volcano. St Patrick is said to have spent the 40 days of Lent here in the year 441 praying for Ireland's deliverance from paganism. Ever since, it has been a place of Christian pilgrimage. It takes about an hour to climb the rough track to the top where the view on a clear day extends south to the mountains and lakes of Connemara, and north across Clew Bay. Clare Island, 8 km (5 miles) offshore, was the stronghold of Grace O'Malley, a pirate queen who went to London to meet Elizabeth I.

Westport

Pretty Westport was laid out in 1780 by James Wyatt, with an octagonal centre and a wide main street leading down to the River Carrowbeg. The 18th-century Westport House has beautiful plasterwork, furniture and paintings, and a children's zoo in the grounds; cold dungeons under the house are all that's left from an earlier castle. At Westport Quay, old warehouses have been given a facelift and turned into restaurants, bars and shops. Westport is a centre for fishing and sailing, and its musicians have made a name for themselves too. The Chieftains' flute player Matt Molloy owns a pub here, and the town stages festivals in July and September.

Newport on Clew Bay is dedicated to sea angling. The Georgian mansion, Newport House, is now a hotel, known for its cooking as well as its elegant interiors.

Achill Island

Ireland's biggest offshore island offers stunning views, vertiginous cliffs and pristine beaches, but the golden eagles which gave the island its name are a rare sight now. Between its rocky mountain slopes and sodden bogs, there was never enough cultivable land, and life in the past was hard. Now, many old cottages have been replaced by spacious modern houses and summer brings a rush of Irish visitors across the bridge from the mainland with sailboards and fishing equipment.

Keel has a long, beautiful beach and a golf course in the dunes. Keel Lough gives novice windsurfers a chance to practise before trying their skills on the bay. The lane inland from Keel leads to the lower slopes of Slievemore, 670 m (2,200 ft). An hour's hard walking will take you to the top where the views to the north are breathtaking. West of Keel, Croghaun is almost as high, and a 550-m (1,900-ft) precipice to the northwest is even more spectacular, forming Europe's highest sea cliffs.

Céide Fields

On exposed cliffs near Ballycastle, farmers slicing into a peat bog began to expose a maze of white stone walls, which proved to be the field boundaries and building left by Neolithic people over 5,000 years ago. The peat had built up as the climate turned worse and blanket bog claimed the area. Paths criss-cross the site and a pyramid-shaped visitor centre explains its importance.

Killala

The stone quays and warehouses of Killala tell of past trade, but the port is mainly a base for fishing these days. A bust of the French General Humbert in the town centre recalls one of the heroic failures of Irish history. He landed at the head of a French expedition in August 1798, too late to support the United Irishmen's rising of that year. Joined by Irish Volunteers, his force took Ballina and defeated local militias at Castlebar, but it was surrounded at Ballinamuck by regular troops and compelled to surrender.

In Ballina, the main focus of interest is the impressive number of salmon in the River Moy. From spring to late summer, you may see fishermen hauling a catch ashore in nets: they've been licensed to take salmon this way for centuries.

Foxford's Woollen Mills was started in 1892 by the Irish Sisters of Mercy to increase local employment, and soon became famous for blankets and tweeds. Some of the fabrics woven today go to top couturiers. You can tour the mill, more mechanized these days, and see some surprising colour combinations that are now woven and soft traditional shades.

Knock

Since 1879, when a vision of the Virgin Mary, St Joseph and St John was seen on the end wall of the village church, Knock has been a place of pilgrimage. Pope John Paul II came for the centenary and hundreds of thousands attended the papal mass. There was no convenient airport at the time, so the local priest, Father Horan, proposed building a runway long enough to take jumbo jets. Somehow the money was raised, and in 1986, Horan International Airport opened. It's not exactly busy but more flights use it than the doubters expected, bringing weekenders and fishing parties as well as a steady flow of pilgrims. The end of the old church has been enclosed by a glass extension, with statues simulating the 1879 vision. A cavernous modern basilica can hold 20,000 people.

County Sligo

You'll soon be made aware that this is *The Land of Heart's Desire* described by W. B. Yeats and his artist brother Jack. But it won't only be their admirers who will want to visit the beauty spots that inspired them. In a gentler landscape than Mayo to the south or Donegal to the north, the massive mountains of Ben Bulben and Knocknarea stand out all the more. No wonder they are woven round with tales of Celtic legend.

Sligo Town

The chief town of the region stands on the River Garavogue between Lough Gill and a broad, sheltered bay. The Norman lords Fitzgerald and de Burgo seized lands in the area in the 13th century; the ruined Dominican Friary in Abbey Street was built at that time and wrecked in 1641 during the Civil War. The town you see now was mainly an Anglo-Irish creation in the 18th and 19th centuries. The tourist office in Temple Street has a map of the sights.

Rohan Gillespie's modern statue of a rumpled W. B. Yeats stands in Stephen Street, north of the river. The poet spent most of his school holidays here and often returned in later life. The County Museum in Stephen Street has a suitable Stone Age bias, given the number of monuments from that

"So red and rosy were her cheeks"—girl from a folksong in a land of music.

era which pepper the region. Naturally the museum has a Yeats Memorial room, with first editions, photographs and letters. The adjoining Library and Municipal Art Gallery has paintings and drawings by Jack B. Yeats, their father John Butler Yeats and Jack's daughter, Anne Yeats, all noted artists. Across the river by Douglas Hyde Bridge, the Yeats Memorial Building has another Yeats collection and an audio-visual display about the writer.

Knocknarea

Looming behind the windswept beach at Strandhill, Knocknarea is a flat-topped mountain 329 m (1,078 ft) high, crowned by a huge cairn, or pile of rock. Legend says it's the grave of Queen Maeve (or *Meadhbh*, one of several Irish spellings). A queen of Connacht in the Amazonian mould, she probably lived in the 1st century AD, but the cairn may be a passage tomb from about 3000 BC, like Newgrange, although no serious excavation has been attempted. The best route up is from the south, a 40-minute walk and worth the effort for the views alone. Once on top you'll appreciate the size of the mound, a truncated cone 200 m (650 ft) round the base, 90 m (300 ft) round the top and 10 m (33 ft) high. The mass of stone in it is estimated at 40,000 tonnes!

Carrowmore

A vast Stone Age cemetery southwest of Sligo comprises dolmens, small passage tombs and stone circles, about 60 in all. They date from 3000 to 2000 BC, and no doubt were positioned for the view of Knocknarea, clearly visible to the west. A walk across green fields takes you to some of the sites, on both sides of the road.

Lough Gill

The lovely lake southeast of Sligo is famous as the setting of Yeats's *The Lake Isle of Innisfree*. Apart from that, there's no special reason to visit the islet itself, although boats which make trips on the lake sometimes stop there. On land, the road on the north shore gives the best views; take the signs for Hazelwood and Half Moon Bay, where there's a sculpture trail with works by Irish and international artists. At the northeast corner of the lake, Parke's Castle is a 17th-century fortified manor, now a regional information centre.

To the south, 22 km (14 miles) from Sligo, Ballymote is known for coarse fishing, folk music and the ruins of the Norman castle built by Richard de Burgo. To the west, Tobercurry is another centre of traditional music, where the celebrated Chieftains made their name.

Rosses Point

With its sandy beaches, golf course and backdrop of purple mountains, Rosses Point is Sligo's seaside resort on the north side of the bay. The flat Coney Island in the mouth of the bay, reached by a causeway at low tide, is a feeding ground for ducks, geese and wading birds. It's claimed that New York's Coney Island was given the same name by a Sligo captain who said the rabbits there reminded him of the Irish original.

Drumcliff

Just as he specified in a poem, the grave of W. B. Yeats stands near the door of Drumcliff church, north of Sligo, and he wrote the epitaph inscribed on the plain headstone:

Cast a cold eye
on life, on death
Horseman, pass by!

Yeats died in 1939 in the south of France, and was temporarily buried at Roquebrune. War delayed arrangements for his body to be brought home, and he was not buried here until September 1948. In the background is Ben Bulben, 527 m (1,730 ft), rearing up like the prow of a great ship.

Lissadell House, north of Drumcliff, with a classical exterior, lofty halls and a columned gallery 30 m (100 ft) long, was the home of the extraordinary Gore-Booth family: Sir Robert, who went into debt to feed the hungry during the famines, Henry, the Arctic explorer, his daughter Eva and her younger sister Constance (Countess Markievicz), a fiery revolutionary who fought in the 1916 Easter Rising. W. B. Yeats was a frequent visitor.

Mullaghmore

Shielded from Atlantic gales by the headland and its harbour, Mullaghmore is a pretty holiday centre. The pinnacled Classiebawn Castle on top of the peninsula was a favourite retreat of Earl Mountbatten, who chose to ignore warnings about security. In 1979, he was killed when his boat was blown up by the IRA. Near the main road, the Creevykeel court tomb is the finest of its kind in Ireland, thought to date from about 3000 BC.

County Donegal

A long, rugged coastline facing the Atlantic culminates in the most northerly point of Ireland at Malin Head. The Normans scarcely penetrated here, and the English hardly more. There's still a substantial Gaelic-speaking minority.

At Ballyshannon, the Republic narrows to a bottleneck as County Fermanagh in Northern Ireland almost reaches to the coast. A

Weaving tweed is still a cottage industry in Donegal and Mayo.

dam has turned the River Erne into a lake stretching almost to the border with Northern Ireland, only 8 km (5 miles) away.

Donegal Town
Donegal was the principal base of the O'Donnell clan, led by the Earl of Tyrconnell. After the Flight of the Earls in 1607, their estates were seized and awarded to English and Scottish colonists. Donegal town went to Sir Basil Brooke, who transformed the 16th-century O'Donnell tower house by putting in big mullioned windows and adding a Jacobean gabled wing. Inland, the pretty Lough Eske is famous for its

fishing. To the west, at the fishing port of Killybegs, the smell of a fishmeal factory pervades the town, and a colourful fleet of trawlers packs the harbour.

Western Peninsula
The road west, tortuous and narrow, is forced away from the coast for much of the way, notably by the cliffs of Slieve League, dropping steeply from the 601-m (1,972-ft) summit to the sea. Its northern slopes are less precipitous, but they are bleak and boggy so the fertile green of Glencolumbkille with its brightly painted houses is all the more welcome. The Glen of St

Colmcille (or Columba) was a favourite with the saint who was born not far away at Lough Gartan (see below). It has been a focus of pilgrimage ever since, although some of today's secular pilgrims spend more time in craft shops than holy places. The valley seems also to have been important in pagan times, judging by the number of tombs from various eras, some of them adapted to Christian purposes: small standing stones and dolmens have been marked with crosses. The information office in the village will provide a map of the sites. On the saint's day, 9 June, hundreds of pilgrims take a similar path, perhaps following in his footsteps.

Ardara, at the head of the bay to the north, is known for knitted woollens and homespun tweed, much of it still made in people's homes. Displays in a visitor centre explain the processes and the history.

Northwest Donegal

Unless you have the luxury of time, you'll have to choose between routes. You might follow every twist and turn of the coast road through tiny Gaelic-speaking fishing villages, or head for Mount Errigal and the Glenveagh National Park.

At the Lakeside Centre at Dunlewy, an old weaver's house, you can see the carding, dyeing, spinning and weaving of local wool to produce the famous Donegal tweed. Young farm animals and a playground keep children happy and boats are available for a trip on the lake. Whenever the clouds lift, Mount Errigal, 752 m (2,466 ft), dominates the view to the north, its slopes shining white not with snow, but quartzite. The walk to the top is worth the effort on a clear day. Glenveagh National Park, almost 10,000 ha (25,000 acres) includes the peaks of Errigal and Slieve Snaght, as well as several loughs. Glenveagh Castle is a Victorian Gothic mansion set in fine gardens on Lough Veagh.

At Lough Gartan, the Colmcille (St Columba) Centre at Church Hill honours the saint with an exhibition on the conversion from paganism to Christianity which he helped to bring about. You can walk to the place where he was born into a chieftain's family in 522, marked by a giant cross, and other sites connected with his life. West of Church Hill village, Glebe Gallery was formed by the artist and collector Derek Hill and given to the Irish nation in 1981. Apart from his own paintings, you can see works by Degas, Renoir, Picasso and Kokoschka, and by the naïve school of artists which he discovered (and in effect 67 founded) on Tory Island off the Donegal coast.

Rathmullan is a small village of pastel-coloured cottages and a ruined abbey. It was from here that the Earls of Tyrone and Tyrconnell and their supporters sailed for Spain in 1607, leading to the confiscation of their lands and the Plantation of Ulster. The Battery by the little harbour, built against the threat of invasion 200 years later in the Napoleonic Wars, houses an exhibition, Flight of the Earls.

Letterkenny at the head of Lough Swilly is the commercial centre and county town of Donegal. The 19th-century Catholic cathedral is the chief landmark, and in August the Folk Festival brings in performers and fans of traditional music and dance.

Grianán of Aileach

On a 244-m (800-ft) summit between Lough Swilly and Derry, near the border with Northern Ireland, stands the ancient stone fort known as the Grianán of Aileach. A road climbs almost all the way; then a short walk takes you to the hilltop site. It dates from some time in the Iron Age, perhaps 500 to 200 BC, although there's evidence of earlier ramparts. Claudius Ptolemy showed it on his famous map of Ireland of the 2nd century AD, drawn from reports he was given by traders. It became a stronghold of the local kings in the early Christian era and St Patrick came to preach. Destroyed around 1100, it was restored in the 19th century. Like the Staigue Fort in County Kerry, it has chambers in the walls and double staircases up to the gallery, which runs round the inside of walls 5 m (16 ft) high.

Inishowen Peninsula

Not quite the island (inis) that its name suggests, the peninsula between Lough Swilly and Lough Foyle is the northernmost tip of Ireland, although not in Northern Ireland. Buncrana is a sheltered loughside resort favoured by holidaymakers from Derry just across the border. At Carndonagh, by the wall of the old church below the village, you'll find a 7th-century cross decorated with Celtic knot designs and with guard stones on either side carved with primitive figures.

Malin Head is as far north as the Irish mainland goes, though from the cliffs you can see the little island of Inishtrahull, deserted since the last inhabitants were taken off in 1930. Several ships of the Spanish Armada came to grief on this coast; the wreck of the Trinidad Valencera was found offshore to the east and some of the objects recovered are on display in the Ulster Museum in Belfast.

NORTHERN IRELAND

Londonderry (Derry), North Coast, Glens of Antrim,
Belfast, Ards Peninsula, St Patrick's Country,
Mourne Mountains, Armagh, County Fermanagh, Omagh

No picture of Ireland is complete without a visit to "the North". The Giant's Causeway is just one of many highlights. Belfast is brightening itself up and transforming its waterfront, and the Ulster Museum is a treasure house of world class. In the west, the Lakes of Fermanagh attract anglers from all over Europe. The border between Northern Ireland and the Republic is almost invisible these days; the European single market means there is little for customs to do.

Londonderry (Derry)

Close to the border with County Donegal in the Republic, the city that most people call Derry had "London" attached when English companies invested in land there in the 17th century. It had been an old monastic site, but little was left when Protestant settlers arrived to build a new town, with strong walls which stand to this day. When James II landed in Ireland in 1689 to try to recapture his throne from William of Orange, young apprentices shut the gates against his troops, an event commemorated by Protestants in the annual Apprentice Boys' March. James's army be-

sieged the city for 105 days until ships broke through a boom which the besiegers had put across the River Foyle.

As Derry industrialized, it attracted people from Donegal, then one of the poorest parts of Ireland, until there was actually a Catholic majority, but the electoral system deprived them of influence. Civil rights marchers clashed with police in 1968 and 1969, and British troops fired on demonstrators on January 31, 1972, killing 13 on what became known as Bloody Sunday. More recently, Derry has led the way in improving relations between the communities.

The focus of the compact walled city is the central square, the Diamond. You can climb up on the city walls and walk along them, past cannon used by the defenders during the siege. Behind the Georgian Court House in Bishop Street, St Columb's Cathedral looks just like an English parish church. (This is the Protestant cathedral: St Eugene's Catholic Cathedral overlooks the Bogside suburbs.) Down near Shipquay Gate, the City Museum occupies O'Doherty's Tower, a replica of a 16th-century tower house. Below the gate, the quay-sides saw the departure of thousands of 19th-century emigrants, driven out by depression in Ulster and famine in the west.

North Coast

Once a centre of the linen industry, Coleraine is the main campus of the University of Ulster. Around Mountsandel Fort to the southeast, flint tools and bone fragments were found, dating from about 7000 BC.

High on the cliffs west of Coleraine, the round, classical Mussenden Temple (1785) was built as a library and summerhouse by an eccentric Bishop of Derry who was also Earl of Bristol. A great traveller, he was famous for demanding the best accommodation, so when the first luxury hotels were created in his wake, many were called Hotel Bristol.

The coastal resorts of Portstewart and Portrush survive on mainly local visitors and golfers who come to the famous links. Portrush occupies north-pointing Ramore Head so it enjoys both east- and west-facing seafronts, with rows of Victorian guesthouses and bracing breezes.

The romantic ruins of Dunluce Castle stand on a rocky promontory, almost cut off by a deep gorge where the drawbridge used to be. The waves have eroded the cliffs below the castle, taking parts of the building too. It was once a stronghold of the Mac-Donnells, but they abandoned it in the 17th century, perhaps put off when the kitchens and several servants fell into the sea.

UNIONISTS AND REPUBLICANS

Northern Ireland is a part of the United Kingdom of Great Britain and Northern Ireland ("UK" for short). Some people call it Ulster, although it comprises only six of the nine counties of the old province of Ulster, those which had a Protestant majority when Ireland was partitioned in 1921. The other 26 counties, with a large Catholic majority, form the Republic of Ireland. Northern Ireland's Protestants, over 60% of the population, overwhelmingly vote for Unionist parties—and by Union they mean the one with Britain. The Catholics just as overwhelmingly support parties that call for a united Ireland. The IRA, illegal on both sides of the border, has used violence in pursuit of its aims, as have the Protestant paramilitaries, also illegal. Britain has promised to preserve the Union as long as a majority in Northern Ireland wish it to do so, but has also promoted closer relations with the Republic.

Old Bushmills Distillery

Since Bushmills was granted a licence to make whiskey in 1608, the process has hardly changed, except in scale, and the water still comes from the same stream. Old malt kilns have been converted into a museum and the Potstill Bar, where you can sample the product after a tour.

Giant's Causeway

Mistaking it for a castle, a ship of the Spanish Armada bombarded it. And legend says the Causeway was built by the giant Finn McCool, the Ulster warrior and king of Ireland's armies, so he could walk to Scotland. It has always been hard to accept that a structure so exact could be natural; even knowing the geological explanation, you'll have the same feeling. Some 60 million years ago, molten rock slowly cooled, contracted and crystallized into 40,000 basalt columns, clustered in terraces at the water's edge. Most are hexagonal, though some have five or seven sides.

An easy path (or shuttle bus) takes you down from the car park on the cliffs. Along the coastal path to the east, round the next headland, Port na Spaniagh (Spanish Inlet) was named after the Armada ship *Girona*, wrecked here in 1588. Some of its treasures are in the Ulster Museum in Belfast.

Rathlin Island

Robert the Bruce is said to have sheltered in a cave on Rathlin in 1306 after his defeat by the English at Perth. It was here that the sight of a spider perseveringly weaving its web inspired him to "try, try, try again". The island is a bird sanctuary now; in good weather motor launches make the 45-minute trip from Ballycastle, a holiday centre with a golf course.

Fair Head

A cliff rearing up to 194 m (636 ft) marks the point where this dramatic coastline turns south. If the weather is clear, the walk to the top pays off with views of Rathlin Island and the coast of Scotland, 21 km (13 miles) away.

Glens of Antrim

South of Cushendun, nine pretty valleys (glens) cut down from the moorland of the Antrim Mountains through wooded hills to the sea. Cushendun, a picturebook village with a harbour and matching whitewashed houses was designed by Clough Williams-Ellis (architect of Portmeirion in Wales) and built in about 1920 for Lord Cushendun and his wife. She was Cornish and wanted to be reminded of her home.

Glenaan, one of the smallest of the glens, runs down to the little port of Cushendall. The waterfalls of Glenariff are reached by a short walk from the glen. On the coast road, Waterfoot comes alive in July with Gaelic games and a folk festival. At the village of Glenarm, the castle was the historic seat of the MacDonnells, Earls of Antrim after they moved from Dunluce. Larne is a terminal for ferries to Scotland.

Carrickfergus

Now only used by pleasure craft and a few fishing boats, Carrickfergus was once the main port on this coast. Dominating the harbour is a massive Norman castle, begun by John de Courcy in the 12th century. Housing an army garrison right up to the 20th, it was kept in good repair while others fell into ruin.

William of Orange landed at Carrickfergus in 1690 on his way to the Battle of the Boyne. A French force seized it in 1760 in a daring raid, and in 1778, the American naval hero John Paul Jones defeated the British ship *HMS Drake* just offshore.

Belfast

Newcomers to Belfast are often agreeably surprised to find a bright, modern city with a vibrant cultural and entertainment scene. The pubs are lively; the people are cheerful and chatty. There is rarely any sign of the troubles which kept Northern Ireland's capital in the news for so long.

The industrial revolution transformed Belfast from a small port into a commercial and manufacturing giant. Its imposing public buildings date from the 19th and early 20th century, when the city was the world's biggest ship-builder and linen manufacturer and a leader in the cotton and tobacco industries. The population explosion that came with this expansion created extensive slums, with separate Protestant and Catholic areas established early in the process.

The Depression of the 1930s hit hard until World War II got the factories working again. German bombing caused enormous damage, but production of ships and aircraft still went up month by month.

After the war, new housing estates were built, mainly on the western edges of the city. Attempts were made to integrate the Protestant and Catholic communities, but these were abandoned after the riots of 1968–69. To this day, areas of different persuasions in West Belfast are separated by high fences, and colourful murals proclaim local allegiances. If you want to visit them, ask at the Northern Ireland Tourist Board in North Street

Belfast's political murals have become a tourist attraction.

about tours of Catholic Falls and Ballymurphy and Protestant Shankill and Crumlin roads.

City Centre

The great copper dome of the 1906 City Hall on Donegall Square is a landmark. Outside by green lawns stand memorials to war dead and the victims of the sinking of the Belfast-built *Titanic*. The area to the north of City Hall is mainly pedestrianized: Royal Avenue and the connecting streets have most of the big shops. North along Donegall Street, St Anne's Cathedral (Church of Ireland) is a solid example of Romanesque revival.

Two Victorian gems have been restored in Great Victoria Street. The 1890s Grand Opera House has a richly gilded interior and the Crown Liquor Saloon is a jewel-box of fine woodwork and brass, engraved glass and tiles, with private boxes ("snugs") and a long bar where you can sample some local oysters and a Guinness.

Waterfront

The banks of the River Lagan, derelict for decades, have been transformed, with the building of the magnificent Waterfront Hall, the Odyssey entertainment complex and international hotels. A weir controls the river so it no longer turns into a mud flat twice a day.

Botanic Gardens

South of the centre along Great Victoria Street, the 1849 buildings of Queen's University look like a Tudor palace. Adjoining them are the Botanic Gardens, a popular public park with superb flower displays and a curvaceous Palm House of cast iron and hundreds of glass panels, older than the one at London's Kew Gardens.

Ulster Museum

Next to the Botanic Gardens, a modern building houses the city's museum and art gallery. The art collection (on the top floor) is international, but Irish artists have pride of place: Roderic O'Conor who was inspired by Van Gogh, Belfast-born Sir John Lavery, Jack B. Yeats and Gerard Dillon. Among the watercolours and drawings, look out for the work of Edward Lear, who would rather have been remembered for his art than his nonsense verse, Samuel Palmer, Rowlandson and Fuseli.

Glass, silver, ceramics and textiles are also on the upper floors. Natural history comes next: geology, flora and fauna, fossils and dinosaur skeletons. Archaeological finds include Neolithic flint tools, Bronze Age gold jewellery and relics from the early Christian era. Treasures recovered from the Spanish ship *Girona*, wrecked near the Giant's Causeway in 1588, include gold jewellery set with precious stones, weapons and domestic objects.

The lower floors cover local history, celebrating Belfast's role in the industrial revolution.

Ulster Folk and Transport Museum

By road or rail along the south shore of Belfast Lough, the Ulster Folk and Transport Museum is about 13 km (8 miles) from the city, near Holywood. Original buildings have been brought from all over the province: houses, a weaver's workshop, forge, school and church. Peat fires burn in the cottages, which are furnished as they might have been over a century ago. Don't miss the Folk Gallery, where exhibitions of early photographs, prints and drawings are mounted.

The Transport Museum's galleries are filled with carriages, veteran cars and railway rolling stock, here put into an Irish context. Particularly unusual are the primitive rural panniers and sleds, and among the cars are a Belfast-built 1906 Chambers and the ill-starred De Lorean of 1982. The section on shipbuilding recalls the days when Belfast led the world. There's a range of models of the aircraft produced by the pioneer Short Brothers, especially their famous flying boats.

Stormont

Off the road to Newtownards, Stormont is the classical palace built in 1928 for the Northern Ireland Parliament. The United Kingdom government in London suspended the parliament in 1972, but the Good Friday agreement of 1998 led to the establishment of a new assembly.

Ards Peninsula

A long finger of land attracts Belfast people to its east-coast beaches when the weather is fine. The sheltered waters of Strangford Lough to the west are good for fishing, windsurfing and bird-watching (the foreshore is a nature reserve). Mount Stewart, facing the lough, was the home of Lord Castlereagh, one of the architects of the treaties that ended the Napoleonic Wars. The Georgian house (a National Trust property) is more modest than many stately homes of that era, but the neoclassical interior is impressive. The gardens are a paradise of formal flowerbeds, vistas and secret corners, dotted with statuary including every mythical animal imaginable.

If you are heading south, there's no need to retrace your journey back up the Ards Peninsula. A passenger and car ferry runs every half-hour from Portaferry to Strangford across the narrow mouth of Strangford Lough. 75

St Patrick's Country

The patron saint of Ireland is believed to have set up his first church in a barn at Saul. A replica of an early church was built in 1932 to mark the 1500th anniversary of his landing in Ireland. He returned many times to Saul, and died there in about 461.

Just out of Strangford, the 18th-century Castle Ward was built with a classical west front and a fanciful "Gothick" east front, reflecting the contrasting tastes of Lord and Lady Bangor. The estate, run by the National Trust, includes formal gardens, a Victorian children's games centre and seashore wildfowl reserve.

Downpatrick was a local chief's stronghold when the Norman lord John de Courcy marched up from Dublin with 300 men and seized it. Earlier, St Patrick is said to have founded a monastery, perhaps on the hill where the Church of Ireland Down Cathedral now stands. Legend claims that he is buried here, but there is no evidence to back up the position of the stone to be seen in the graveyard.

Mourne Mountains

As the song goes, they "sweep down to the sea". More to the point, the mountains rise steeply out of gentle countryside to provide excellent hill-walking. The highest peak in Ulster, Slieve Donard, 852 m (2,796 ft), stands on the outskirts of Newcastle, an old-established seaside resort. Starting in Donard Park, the track to the summit is a vigorous walk rather than a climb, and the view from the hermit's cell at the top can be superb, taking in the Isle of Man, southwest Scotland and the Antrim Mountains.

Armagh

This compact city has been the religious capital of all Ireland since St Patrick established his bishopric here in the 5th century. A circle of streets follows the lines of ancient walls, with the

4

FOUR BEAUTIFUL GARDENS Ireland's temperate climate helped former landowners create some superb gardens: at **Powerscourt** near Dublin the great house has gone, but the garden survives; **Tully** near Kildare has an authentic Japanese Garden; frost-free **Garinish Island** in Bantry Bay is an Italian garden; and **Mount Stewart** on the Ards Peninsula in Northern Ireland is lovingly tended by the National Trust.

Anglican St Patrick's Cathedral on a hill at the centre, perhaps the site of the saint's own church. The present building dates mainly from the 18th century. King Brian Boru, who drove the Norsemen out of Ireland in 1014, is buried in the church graveyard.

On a hillside to the northwest, the Perpendicular-style Catholic St Patrick's Cathedral was finished in 1873; its striking interior shines with brilliantly coloured mosaics. Some public buildings and town houses survive from the 18th century, particularly around the Mall, formerly a racecourse.

Navan Fort

West of Armagh City across the River Callan, grass-covered ramparts 230 m (750 ft) across ring a huge mound. There is little doubt that this was the ancient capital of Ulster, Emain Macha, from the 4th century BC to the 4th century AD. Excavations have shown that in 94 BC a great wooden temple was built on the mound and, within the year, set on fire and burnt out, perhaps a funeral pyre.

In the Loughnashade lake near the mound, 200 years ago, a farmer discovered four 2,000-year-old bronze trumpets and several human skulls. A visitor centre provides some background information and displays of jewellery, weapons and tools found on the site.

County Fermanagh

Enniskillen grew up on an island site where Upper and Lower Lough Erne meet. The old castle, given a Scottish look by 17th-century settlers, houses local and military museums. The Doric column above the town is a monument to Sir Galbraith Lowry Cole, one of Wellington's generals who was born here. In summer, you can climb its 108 steps to the top for a view of the town and lakes. On the southeastern outskirts, Castlecoole is a magnificent neoclassical mansion built in 1798 by James Wyatt for the Earl of Belmore.

The border town of Belleek is noted for a curious kind of china made to look like basketware which you'll see in shops all over Ireland. The pottery welcomes visitors to its museum.

Lakes of Fermanagh

With a combined length of 80 km (50 miles), Lower and Upper Lough Erne form a maze of waterways, islands, inlets and reed beds straddling the border. Visitors come from all over Europe to fish. Boats can be hired by the day or week to go fishing or just cruising.

The Palladian mansion of Castle Archdale was demolished but the stable block remains, set in a forest park and housing a natural history museum. The now tran-

quil waters of Lough Erne were home to flying boats of the RAF which patrolled the North Atlantic during World War II. A special part of the museum tells their story.

Strange carvings from the pagan and Christian eras have been found on many of the islands in Lower Lough Erne. On White Island, seven intriguing stone figures and a later head are now set in a row in the walls of a ruined church. Only waist-high, with a primitive look and round, staring eyes, they probably date from the 6th to 8th centuries.

Just north of Enniskillen, on Devenish Island, are the extensive ruins of a monastery said to have been founded by St Molaise in the 6th century. The tall 12th-century round tower is unusual for its decorated frieze. There's a boat service to the island in summer.

Omagh

The town is notable for two purpose-built attractions on its outskirts. The Ulster-American Folk Park highlights the connections between this part of Ireland and North America. In the 18th and early 19th centuries, a quarter of a million people left Ulster to make new homes across the Atlantic, and at least ten US presidents, including Andrew Jackson and Woodrow Wilson, traced their ancestry to Ulster. The exhibition hall at the entrance houses frequently changing displays. Armed with a plan of the park, it's best to follow the numerical sequence, starting with typical buildings of early 19th-century Ulster. Some are replicas, some have been brought from other places and reassembled, like the little schoolhouse which seems as if the pupils have only just left. they are all furnished and looked after by staff dressed in the clothes of the period.

You make your way past the shops of an Ulster street to the "dockside" to board the sailing ship *Union*, bound for Baltimore, and—in a great piece of theatre—disembark to emerge in an American street. Buildings on this side include wooden farm buildings complete with live pigs, hens and turkeys.

The Ulster History Park north of Omagh is the most ambitious project of its kind in Ireland. Amid superb landscaping are full scale models of Neolithic houses, a stone circle and tombs, a *crannóg*, an early monastic settlement with church and round tower, a Norman motte-and-bailey castle, a working watermill and "plantation" houses of the 17th century.

Under a fickle sky, the Ulster countryside is a welcome green.

79

CULTURAL NOTES

Wizards with Words. In Ireland they are in love with the sound of words, spending them like newly minted coins. No other city in the world can yet equal Dublin's three winners of the Nobel Prize for Literature: George Bernard Shaw, W. B. Yeats and Samuel Beckett, who are honoured today in the country of their birth as they never were in their lifetime. So is the most original writer of English not to have received the prize, James Joyce, whose work was long banned in Ireland. Joyce was not alone in attracting the fury of his compatriots. The plays of Sean O'Casey, now regarded as classics, were frequently drowned by howls of protest.

There are no rules for Irish writers. Many of the famous names celebrated today would not even have recognized themselves as Irish: the 18th-century satirist Jonathan Swift and playwrights Oliver Goldsmith *(She Stoops to Conquer)* and Richard Brinsley Sheridan *(The School for Scandal)* were part of the Anglo-Irish supremacy. So was the greatest wit of his time, Oscar Wilde, who soon moved to London and rarely returned. Joyce, now so revered, left Dublin in 1904 when he was 22 and never lived there again. And Beckett wrote mainly in French, the language of his adopted home.

William Butler Yeats (1865–1939) based his early plays on Celtic mythology, with the aim of reviving a national literature and theatre. His poetry explored the realms of astrology, symbolism and the supernatural, but into all his work was woven the theme of Irish independence. Aware that his writing had influenced the risings of 1916 and 1920–22, he wrote: "because I helped wind the clock, I come to hear it strike".

Music in the Air. You can't travel far in Ireland without hearing music that could only be Irish. Its roots go deep. Ancient instruments have been found preserved in peat bogs, some of them dating from the Bronze Age, over 3,000 years ago. Horns up to 1.5 m (5 ft) long were discovered in excellent condition, complete with flute section and mouthpiece. Still played today, the small single-sided drum called a *bodhran* is another survivor from prehistory, and the traditional Irish harp is a symbol of the nation which has appeared on old coins and coats of arms for more than a thousand years. The sound of an Irish folk band comes from the combination of bagpipes, flute and violin (usually called the fiddle). The *uilleann* pipes differ from Scottish bagpipes in being pumped by bellows squeezed between the player's hip and elbow; the flute carries many a merry jig or wistful lament, while the fiddle—generally solo—cuts a virtuoso dash. Bands such as the Chieftains have opened the ears of the world to traditional Irish folk music, appearing in concerts from the steps of the US Capitol to the Great Wall of China.

Irish songs were long ago carried everywhere that emigrants went, especially influencing Australian folk song and American country-and-western, which in turn has come back to Ireland as a popular import. And today an unmistakable Irishness pervades all kinds of new music. Heard on the sound-tracks of major films and TV commercials, Donegal's Enya creates ethereal sounds all by herself in her studio, recording multiple layers of her own voice with electronic backing. Irish groups and solo artists are prominent on the rock and pop scene; Ireland has won the Eurovision song contest so often it's almost embarrassing. Just as Irish pubs have spread round the world, so has the sound of Irish music.

Two Tongues. Ireland's ancient Gaelic is the official language of the Republic, with English as the accepted practical alternative. Signs and documents are generally bilingual, although car number plates only give the Gaelic name of their place of origin (*Baile Atha Cliath* means Dublin, and *Luimneach* is Limerick). Perhaps you'll be surprised to learn that you already know some Gaelic? Maybe just a "smidgen", from *smeachán*, a little. The opposite term "galore" has moved a long way from *go leír*, which just means enough.

Many terms for landscape features have made the transition: bog from the Gaelic for soft; drumlin from *druimlin*, a small hill; glen, a valley; lough, a lake or sea inlet. One for the specialists, an esker is a ridge left by a glacier, from the Gaelic *eiscir*.

Many a sentimental ballad praises a sweet colleen, from *cailín*, a country girl. And when an Australian male refers to a woman as a "sheila" he's using the girl's name *Síle* which became a generic term. A spalpeen (*spailpín*) was an itinerant worker but came to mean a rascal, one who probably drank poteen (*poitín*, illegally distilled liquor) in a shebeen (*sibín*, an unlicensed bar).

The oddest derivation of all may be that of the word tory, for a Conservative politician or voter. *Tóraí* was Gaelic for an outlaw, especially one who supported the Jacobite cause in the 17th century. Transferred to the Jacobites in the British Parliament, it was eventually inherited by today's Conservative party.

81

Shopping

Like most places with a substantial tourist trade, Ireland has no shortage of souvenir shops, selling much the same things wherever you go: dolls in traditional dress, reproductions of old crosses and costume jewellery using Celtic motifs. There is a lively craft movement too, producing attractive pottery, glass and textiles. And if you've developed a taste for Irish music, there is a vast selection of CDs and tapes to choose from.

You might expect free trade within the European Union to mean that prices would be much the same on both sides of the border. In practice there's often a substantial difference, caused by differing tax rates and exchange rate fluctuations between the Irish punt and the pound sterling. Many things are cheaper in Northern Ireland, attracting shoppers from the Republic; in other cases the reverse is true, as with petrol (gasoline) and diesel fuel.

Although Galway, Kilkenny, Wexford and other provincial centres have charmingly old-fashioned shops, only the two capitals can offer a wide choice. In Dublin, the big stores and international names are concentrated on Grafton Street and along O'Connell Street, with more specialist shops in the side streets leading off them. For books, antiques and junk, wander through the lanes of Temple Bar and further west in the Liberties district.

Belfast's biggest department stores are found around Donegall Place and Royal Avenue, with speciality shops in Cornmarket, Fountain Street and the covered arcades. St George's Market operates on Friday mornings in May Street. Bookshops around Queens University, south of the centre, are the place to look for old and new books. The shops at the Ulster Museum and the Ulster Folk and Transport Museum are good sources of gifts and souvenirs, such as books, model-making kits and reproductions of paintings by Irish artists.

What to Buy

Creative crafts are flourishing; for good original designs in metal-work, ceramics and glass, look in the Kilkenny Design Centre (it also has a branch in Dublin), the

Cork Design Centre and the craft shops of St Stephen's Green Centre in Dublin. Waterford is the best-known name for both cut glass (crystal) and blown glass, but it has competition from other factories and many small workshops. Potteries large and small

make everything from plant pots to unique artworks. The Belleek factory in County Fermanagh makes china ornaments in pastel colours and characteristic basket-like designs, sold all over Ireland.

Traditional crafts such as basketry, lace-making and woodworking have been revived. Ornaments carved from jet-black bog oak, preserved for thousands of years in peat bogs, were a favourite souvenir with 19th-century visitors; you can find antique and modern examples.

Jewellers make use of Celtic patterns in enamel and silver brooches and earrings. The Claddagh ring is a clasped hands-and-heart design, originally from Galway but now found everywhere.

Hand-knitted or machine-made woollen knitwear can be a good buy. Aran sweaters in natural wool are never out of fashion, and can be found on sale all over the west of Ireland as well as in the big city stores. Knitters on the Aran Islands can't keep up with the demand, but mainland workers make a product of equal quality.

Tweed is still hand-woven in the cottages of Mayo and Donegal, and in a few old-established mills. But the product range has changed: lighter, finer fabrics and eye-catching colours are in demand by the fashion industry, as well as soft blends with cashmere and mohair.

Northern Ireland is the traditional home of fine linen, and although very little flax is grown now, the fabric is still produced —and some is imported as well. From the luxury of pure linen bedsheets to a souvenir tea-towel printed with an Irish motif, the choice is wide.

Some Irish foods are packed ready to travel, notably smoked salmon, delicatessen items and preserves. You will pay more at the airport than if you buy in a high street store. The reverse is true for Irish whiskey and other spirits (liquor) which really do cost less at the duty-free shops. Shannon has a particularly good selection of goods.

83

Dining Out

There is no shortage of top-quality ingredients: oysters, scallops, crabs and mussels from the sea loughs, salmon and trout from the rivers, beef and lamb reared on green pastures, tasty farmhouse cheeses. A wide selection of fruits, vegetables and salads is available since EU membership encouraged year-round imports from the sunny Mediterranean.

Until recent years it was hard to find a good restaurant in Ireland; overcooking was the rule and frying the usual method. The wonderful seafood was mostly exported to France, Spain or anywhere it was appreciated. Now all that has changed. Chefs have become adventurous and creative; many of them have worked in the hotel business around the world and returned full of ideas. Their customers, used to taking their holidays abroad, are more demanding. The cities, especially Dublin, have some fine restaurants; so do holiday centres such as Kinsale, Dingle and Galway; and many of the country house hotels are justly proud of their food.

Pub food can be excellent, or dull; the best pubs can produce fresh, appetizing sandwiches, salads and tasty grills. Chinese, Indian and other ethnic restaurants widen the choice and the usual fast foods are available, headed by fish and chips.

Traditional Irish cooking is mainly found in the home, but turns up on some menus in the form of thick soups or an Irish stew (mutton or lamb chops, carrots, onions, herbs and of course potatoes). Dublin coddle combines bacon, sausage, potatoes, onions and parsley, while colcannon is a meatless stew of potatoes, onions and cabbage.

Breakfast

Stick to continental frugality if you like, but the room rate in most places includes an "Irish breakfast" of fruit juice, porridge or cereal, bacon, egg and sausage, and toast. In the north, you may be offered an "Ulster fry", a huge plateful of bacon, sausage, fried egg, tomato, mushrooms, black pudding (blood sausage), fried potatoes and fried bread. Another filling treat, soda bread is a moist,

It won't take you long to acquire a taste for the black stuff.

grainy bread made with whole-wheat flour and sour milk, using bicarbonate of soda instead of yeast to make it rise.

Cheeses

The big Irish dairy industry used to produce little more than a plain cheddar-type cheese, dyed orange to suit local preference. Now there's a good choice of hard and soft varieties, and some superb farmhouse cheeses mainly to be found in the better restaurants. Look for Cashel Blue from Tipperary, semi-soft Gubbeen from west Cork, Knockalara made from sheep's milk and a tempting range of goatsmilk cheeses.

Desserts

Pastries, pies and ice creams are the mainstays, but where Irish traditions are being revived, you may be offered something unique. Carrageen moss is a seaweed rich in minerals and containing a natural jelling agent. Washed and dried, it's then boiled with milk to make a delicate jelly, served with fruit and cream.

Drinks

A wide range of beers is available, including imports, but stout is the local favourite, whether Guinness or another brewer's brand, such as the slightly sweeter Murphy's or Beamish. If 85 you'd like to try one, ask for "a Guinness" (that means a pint) or "a glass of Guinness" (a half-pint) and prepare to wait while the ritual unfolds. The barman or barmaid will partly fill your glass—up to about four-fifths—and leave it for a few minutes. While you wait, you can watch a phenomenon that appears to contradict the laws of physics; the bubbles seem to *fall* through the liquid. (It took a recent scientific study to discover the explanation. Most bubbles rise up the middle of the glass, carrying liquid with them; some of that then flows down inside the sides of the glass, taking the smaller bubbles with it.) Then the glass is topped off, leaving a thumb's thickness of creamy foam dense enough to write your name in, contrasting with the nearly black drink beneath.

Apart from the 'e', Irish whiskey differs from Scotch in another way: in the malting process the sprouted barley is heated indirectly, avoiding the taste imparted by peat smoke. All five main brands produced in the Republic of Ireland come from one huge French-owned (!) distillery at Midleton in County Cork; the different flavours result from the proportion of malted barley and the kind of barrels used to store the spirit. In Northern Ireland, the Bushmills whiskey distillery claims to hold the world's oldest licence, dating from 1608.

Even those who don't drink whiskey may enjoy it in an Irish coffee. To make one, put a measure of Irish in a large wine glass, add brown sugar and hot black coffee, stir, and then float thick whipped cream on top.

Wine lists cover the world, although taxes keep prices high, and all the usual brands of soft drinks are available.

STAPLE DIET

The potato became an Irish staple in the 17th century, when it was found how well the climate suited it; unlike cereal crops, no dry spell was needed for the harvest. The poor in the rural west came to rely almost entirely on potatoes, so when the crop repeatedly failed from blight in the 1840s, famine was inevitable. Potatoes are still a mainstay of Irish cooking, in stews, baked, roasted, mashed or as chips (french fries). An Ulster speciality is potato bread, or "fadge", made from mashed potato, grated raw potato, flour, buttermilk and seasonings, rolled into flat cakes and baked on a griddle. It can turn up as part of a cooked breakfast, or spread with butter and jam for afternoon tea.

Sport and Activities

Ireland is not the place for a seaside holiday; the beaches may be beautiful but the weather is uncertain and the sea too cold. Those in search of action have plenty of other options. And even if you don't share their love of horses, there's no better way to see the Irish at play than spending a day at the races.

Walking

The best way to enjoy the mountain and coastal scenery is on foot, if you're well prepared. For anything more than a short stroll, wear strong, comfortable shoes, carry raingear and check the weather forecast before you set out. Especially in the mountains of the west, paths are few and tempting expanses of hillside can turn out to be impenetrable bogs. Buy the appropriate Ordnance Survey map, take local advice and don't go alone into the remoter parts. And if you don't feel like climbing hills, you can follow canal towpaths or the banks of the Boyne or the Shannon.

Cycling

The mainly quiet country roads and the short distances from place to place make cycling a good way to see the country. Bicycles can be rented by the day or the week at most holiday centres, and some hotels provide them for their guests. Increasingly popular are the package holidays that let you pedal at your own speed from one good hotel to the next, while a van carries your baggage.

On Horseback

The most popular form of equestrian holiday, trail-riding comes in two main forms: you can be based in one place and take a different route each day; or stay at a different farmhouse or guesthouse each night. The Tourist Board publishes lists of the centres that offer trail rides through all the most scenic areas of the country.

If you want to learn, or to improve your skills, riding centres run residential and non-residential classes.

Fishing

Plenty of regular visitors to Ireland just go to one place, stay there and fish. Coarse fishing in lakes and rivers is excellent; trout

Seasoned golfers claim that Lahinch (founded in 1892) is one of Ireland's most delightful courses.

are plentiful and salmon, although reduced in numbers, still make their way up the rivers. Sea-anglers can fish for pollack, bass, skate and many other species, from the shore or from one of the boats for hire in ports all round the coast. The Tourist Boards publish booklets with details of licences required, costs, where the various species can be found and lists of fishing schools offering instruction at all levels. They will also help you find accommodation where the hosts are used to anglers' ways, ready to dry their clothes, feed them at odd hours and even to smoke a salmon if they catch one.

Golf

The lush parkland courses and breezy coastal links are rated as some of the most beautiful and challenging in the world. The Old Course at Ballybunion in County Kerry is Tom Watson's favourite; Lahinch on a headland in County Clare was built by Scots who wanted to be reminded of St Andrews. Royal Portrush on the north coast is the only course in Ireland to have hosted the British Open. Green fees are low by international standards.

On the Water

Wind-surfing has conquered the world, it seems, and the wetsuit has made it feasible here too. Sheltered loughs are good for beginners' classes, and the waves and winds of the open sea can be a tough test for experts. Daredevil surfers also head for the Atlantic beaches to ride the rollers.

The estuaries and loughs are studded with sails when the weather cooperates, and the rivers are ideal for canoeing holidays. The less energetic can take a cruise for a day, a week or longer on the Shannon, the canal system or the Lakes of Fermanagh.

Spectator Sports

Going to the races is wonderful entertainment, and many of the courses are located in beautiful rural settings. Leopardstown near Dublin has regular meetings, and The Curragh near Kildare is the home of the Irish classics. The flat racing season lasts from March to November, and steeple-chasing—claimed to have been invented in Ireland—runs all year.

Rugby football is another local passion. Famous for its hell-for-leather—and erratic—style of play, the team which plays in the Six Nations championship and other internationals has always been drawn from the whole island. Home matches are played at the Lansdowne Road ground in Dublin but you'll find tickets easier to come by for club and regional games.

Two quintessentially Irish sports are even more like open warfare than rugby, and actually served to keep nationalist fires burning when political avenues were closed. Hurling is a hybrid of hockey and lacrosse, only faster and more dangerous, and Gaelic football has some of the elements of rugby but resembles Australian Rules football.

FIVE SCENIC WALKING ROUTES Coastal paths, mountain tracks, country lanes and canal towpaths are an invitation to walk. For serious hikers, the Tourist Boards have designated and marked several routes, including the **Wicklow Way** through the mountains near Dublin, the **Kerry Way** round the Ring of Kerry, the **Burren Way** in County Clare, the **Western Way** through the wilds of Connemara and Mayo, and the **Ulster Way** along the spectacular northern coast. Each of these would take days to complete, but you can pick sections as short as you please.

The Hard Facts

Airports

Dublin International Airport (DUB) is only 8 km (5 miles) north of the city centre. Airport buses run every 15–20 minutes and take 25 minutes.

Shannon Airport on the west coast (SNN) is 26 km (16 miles) northwest of Limerick. Airport buses run to and from the city every hour and take 30 minutes.

Belfast International Airport (BFS) is 29 km (18 miles) northwest of the city centre. Airport buses run every 30 minutes and take 35 minutes.

Cork, Waterford and some other regional airports also have direct flights to cities in the UK.

All international airports have duty-free shops, banks, bars, restaurants and cafeterias, car rental and information desks.

Baggage

On most flights, the allowance for check-in baggage is 20 kg (44 lb). One small carry-on bag is permitted.

Car Rental

Hiring a car is a quite expensive but convenient way of getting around. Most of the big international companies are represented in Ireland, but to get the best deal it may be worth making a reservation through one of them in your home country, before your visit. Good local companies also operate from airports and main cities, but whichever you use, check that rates include full insurance against loss and damage, and local taxes. There is usually no limit on the distance you can cover, but an extra charge may be levied for drop-off at a different location, and for additional driver(s).

To rent a car, you need a current driving licence and to be over 21 (25 with some companies). You are expected to pay with a major credit card.

Climate

The key word is unpredictable. The average daytime temperature in Dublin in summer is 19°C (66°F); it is seldom hot, and quite frequently cool and wet. The west of Ireland is even more changeable, and wetter. A day which starts sunny will often turn to rain, but conversely if it's pouring when you get up, the sky could be cloudless by midday.

Clothing

Take a raincoat, a rain hat or umbrella, and strong, comfortable walking shoes for sightseeing. Some restaurants in the big cities ask men to wear a jacket and tie, otherwise the Irish are quite informal.

Communications

The telephone system is modern and works well. To make an international call to the Republic of Ireland, dial the international access code followed by the country code (353) and then the area code and number. For Northern Ireland the country code is 44, as for the rest of the UK, and the area code 028.

To make an international call from Ireland, dial 00 and then the country code (1 for US and Canada, 44 for UK), area code (omitting initial zero) and number. There are plenty of coin- and card-operated phones; cards can be bought at post offices, newsagents and some petrol stations.

Digital mobile phones work well almost everywhere; before leaving home, check with your service provider for compatibility.

It generally costs much more to use the phone in your hotel room, unless you use one of the calling cards issued by international telephone companies. E-mail access is available from hotel rooms in the bigger and more modern hotels. Fax messages can be sent and received through most hotels and business service bureaux.

Postal services are good. Air-mail reaches most European destinations in three to five days.

Crime

Ireland is one of the world's safer destinations, but street crime has been on the increase in the cities, fuelled as in most places by a growing drug problem. Just take normal precautions: avoid dark or lonely places at night, and don't leave anything desirable on show when parking your car or leaving it overnight.

Driving

Traffic keeps to the *left*. If you are not used to this, it will soon become familiar, but stay alert; it is easy to set off on the wrong side of the road after making a stop, especially overnight. Watch out on narrow country roads for wandering animals and erratic drivers who don't bother with signals—they expect everyone to know where they are going.

Most road signs in the republic have gone metric, although some in the rural areas have not yet changed. Speed limits are 50 kph (31 mph) in towns, 96 kph (60 mph) out of town and 110 kph (70 mph) on motorways and dual carriageways (divided highways) unless other limits are posted. Low-beam headlights are mandatory during mist and heavy rain. Drivers and passengers must wear seat belts; small children must use a suitable restraint. A red warning triangle, first-aid kit and spare bulbs for the lights should be carried in the vehicle.

Driving under the influence of alcohol or drugs is a serious offence. The alcohol limit is the equivalent of two *small* drinks; to exceed it is to risk a prison sentence.

Not all petrol (gas) stations accept credit cards.

Emergencies

To call the Police, Fire or Ambulance Services dial 999 or 112, and tell the operator which service you require.

Etiquette

People usually shake hands when meeting and taking leave. Friendly informality is the Irish style, with the use of first names being the norm. Even so, business is business and punctuality is expected. The exchange of business cards is especially useful, as many Irish names have unusual spellings and may be pronounced in unexpected ways.

Formalities

British and Irish citizens do not need a passport to travel between the UK and the Republic of Ireland; some form of identification may be needed. Visas are not needed by travellers from western European countries, Australia, Canada, the USA and many other countries.

There is no limit on the import of local or foreign currency.

You may take the following into Ireland duty-free when arriving from non-EU countries: 200 cigarettes or 50 cigars or 250 g tobacco; 1 litre of spirits (liquor) and 2 litres of wine; 50 g of perfume and 250 g of eau de toilette. You must be aged 17 or more to import alcoholic drinks or tobacco products.

Travellers within the EU may import any reasonable quantities of *duty-paid* goods, provided they are for their own use.

No fresh meat or dairy products may be imported.

Health and Medical Matters

It is advisable to take out comprehensive travel insurance, including coverage of medical expenses. Citizens of most western European countries can get free emergency treatment; it helps if they carry a qualifying document (for UK citizens the Form E111 obtainable from post offices before leaving home). Keep receipts for any payments you have to make, in order to claim refunds.

Pharmacies sell a wide variety of medications, but some will be under unfamiliar names. Take with you any medicines you may need—the same brands may not be available. Insect repellent is useful in summer, especially if you are going fishing or cruising on the rivers. You will also need sunscreen.

Tap water is safe to drink everywhere, although some people prefer bottled water.

Language

In the Republic of Ireland, the official language is actually Irish Gaelic, but although it is taught in schools and appears on signs and government documents (with an English version too), very few people have a working knowledge of it. Virtually everyone speaks English, although with a wide variety of regional accents. Only in the *Gaeltacht*, a few pockets of land in the south and west, is the old tongue really alive.

Media

State-run and commercial TV channels are augmented in many hotels by satellite and cable channels, including UK domestic programmes, BBC World, CNN, Sky News, German, French and Italian channels.

As well as the flourishing local press, the London newspapers (some in special Irish editions) are on sale on the morning of publication and other major European newspapers arrive in the main cities by early evening.

Money

The currency is the *punt* or Irish pound (IEP or IR£), divided into 100 pence (p), with banknotes from 5 to 100 pounds and coins from 1p to 1 pound.

The Republic of Ireland is part of the Euro zone, with Euro notes and coins circulating from 1 January 2002.

Northern Ireland, as part of the United Kingdom, uses the pound sterling (GBP or £). There are special Northern Ireland banknotes which are interchangeable with Bank of England notes. Don't confuse them with Irish punts, which are not equivalent.

Foreign currency and traveller's cheques may be changed at banks, exchange offices, large post offices and the bigger hotels (at a poorer rate). Major credit cards are widely accepted. Using them or bank cards, cash may be obtained from cashpoints outside banks, if you know the PIN (personal identification number).

Opening Hours

Museums and other attractions generally open from 9.30 or 10 a.m. to about 4 or 5 p.m. Some close on Monday. It is worth trying to find out in advance.

Shops open from 9 a.m. to 5 or 5.30 p.m., Monday to Saturday.

Some big stores and shopping centres open late on Thursday evenings and from 2 to 6 p.m. on Sunday.

Post offices open from 9 a.m. to 5 p.m., Monday to Friday, 9 a.m. to 1 p.m. Saturday.

Banks open from 10 a.m. to 4 p.m., Monday to Friday. In Northern Ireland they are open from 9.30 a.m. to 4.30 p.m. (and some branches in cities also open on Saturday mornings).

Photography and Video

Film for colour prints can be bought almost anywhere; film for transparencies is sold in larger pharmacies and photographic shops. Colour prints can be quickly processed locally but transparency film is best taken back to your own country for processing. Video-tape is widely available. Pre-recorded tapes are compatible with most of Europe, but not the US.

Public Holidays

If a holiday falls on a Saturday or Sunday, the following Monday is taken as a public holiday.

January 1   New Year's Day
March 17   St Patrick's Day
December 25 Christmas
December 26 St Stephen's Day/
                 Boxing Day

Moveable:
Good Friday (March–April)
Easter Monday (March–April)

Republic of Ireland only
First Monday in June
First Monday in August
Last Monday in October

Northern Ireland only
First Monday in May
Last Monday in May
12 July
Last Monday in August

Public Transport

Taxis are readily available but only those in the bigger cities use meters.

Bus services run regularly within the cities and large towns. Éireann-Irish Bus operates a nationwide network and Ulsterbus covers Northern Ireland and the border towns.

Trains link Dublin with the main cities but since the lines fan out like spokes from the capital, rail travel is rarely practical between provincial centres. Northern Ireland Railways connect Belfast with the larger towns of the north, and across the border to Dublin. Regular domestic flights connect the major airports.

Religion

In the Republic of Ireland most people belong to the Catholic Church, although in recent years attendance has been falling. Other Christian sects and other religions are also represented; services are listed in weekend newspapers.

There is also a large Catholic presence in Northern Ireland, even though the majority of the population there is Protestant, divided between Presbyterian, Church of Ireland and other denominations.

Tax-free Shopping
If you have come from somewhere outside the EU, and you are going to leave it again, you can avoid paying the VAT (sales tax) which ranges from 12.5 to over 20 per cent. The concession applies to major purchases of goods you are taking home or having shipped. Ask at a shop showing the Tax-Free sign how the system works and be sure to obtain proper receipts.

Time
Ireland is on GMT (UTC), advancing to GMT + 1 for daylight saving time from the end of March to the end of October. Thus it is on the same time as the UK, one hour behind most of western Europe, and five hours ahead of east USA and Canada.

Tipping
A service charge is included in most restaurant bills, but an extra 5–10% can always be added for especially good service. Porters are generally tipped about 50p to IR£1 per bag. Taxi fares may be rounded up by about 10 per cent.

Toilets
Clean public lavatories are provided at rail and main bus stations, department stores and some tourist sites. The signs on the doors are often in Irish Gaelic; note that *Mna* means Women, *Fir* means Men.

Tourist Information
The Irish Tourist Board *(Bord Fáilte)* and the Northern Ireland Tourist Board sensibly work together and distribute each other's literature. Their websites are, respectively:

http://www.ireland.travel.ie
http://ni-tourism.com

See inside back cover for addresses and phone numbers.

All major towns have a Tourist Information Office, generally open from 9 a.m. to 4 p.m., Monday to Saturday. Most of them have excellent information leaflets and maps of the local area, as well as a comprehensive list of all kinds of accommodation. Some of the offices in smaller or more remote places are open in summer only.

Voltage
The electrical supply is 220V, 50 Hz, AC. Plugs are of the square, three-pin type, as used in Britain. Apart from shavers for which a marked outlet is provided, any 110V equipment needs a transformer as well as an adaptor.

INDEX

GENERAL EDITOR:
Barbara Ender-Jones
EDITOR:
Christina Grisewood
LAYOUT:
Luc Malherbe
PHOTO CREDITS:
B. Joliat, front cover;
pp. 37 (top), 78;
Hémisphères/Frances, back
cover, p. 66;
/Wysocki, pp. 4, 45, 50, 58;
/Rieger, p. 6; /Colin, p. 10;
/Barbier, p. 31; /Frilet, p. 63;
/Boisvieux, p. 73;
Visa/Lorgnier, pp. 1, 14, 40,
83, 85, 88; /Parinet, p. 55;
D. Laverrière, pp. 18, 26;
M. Kirchgessner, p. 23;
M. Gostelow, p. 37
MAPS:
Huber Kartographie;
Elsner & Schichor

Copyright © 2000
by JPM Publications S.A.
12, avenue Wilaim-Fraisse,
1006 Lausanne, Switzerland
E-mail:
information@jpmguides.com
Web site:
http://www.jpmguides.com/

Printed in Switzerland
Weber/Bienne (CTP)